Beginning BBC micro:bit

A Practical Introduction to micro:bit Development

Pradeeka Seneviratne

Apress®

Beginning BBC micro:bit: A Practical Introduction to micro:bit Development

Pradeeka Seneviratne
Mulleriyawa, Sri Lanka

ISBN-13 (pbk): 978-1-4842-3359-7   ISBN-13 (electronic): 978-1-4842-3360-3
https://doi.org/10.1007/978-1-4842-3360-3

Library of Congress Control Number: 2018930256

Cover image designed by Freepik

Managing Director: Welmoed Spahr
Editorial Director: Todd Green
Acquisitions Editor: Natalie Pao
Development Editor: James Markham
Technical Reviewer: Michael Rimicans
Coordinating Editor: Jessica Vakili
Copy Editor: Kezia Endsley
Compositor: SPi Global
Indexer: SPi Global
Artist: SPi Global

Distributed to the book trade worldwide by Springer Science+Business Media New York, 233 Spring Street, 6th Floor, New York, NY 10013. Phone 1-800-SPRINGER, fax (201) 348-4505, e-mail orders-ny@springer-sbm.com, or visit www.springeronline.com. Apress Media, LLC is a California LLC and the sole member (owner) is Springer Science + Business Media Finance Inc (SSBM Finance Inc). SSBM Finance Inc is a **Delaware** corporation.

For information on translations, please e-mail rights@apress.com, or visit http://www.apress.com/rights-permissions.

Apress titles may be purchased in bulk for academic, corporate, or promotional use. eBook versions and licenses are also available for most titles. For more information, reference our Print and eBook Bulk Sales web page at http://www.apress.com/bulk-sales.

Any source code or other supplementary material referenced by the author in this book is available to readers on GitHub via the book's product page, located at www.apress.com/978-1-4842-3359-7. For more detailed information, please visit http://www.apress.com/source-code.

Printed on acid-free paper

Table of Contents

About the Author

Pradeeka Seneviratne is a software engineer with over 10 years of experience in computer programming and systems design. He is an expert in the development of Arduino and Raspberry Pi-based embedded systems and is currently a full-time embedded software engineer working with embedded systems and highly scalable technologies. Previously, Pradeeka worked as a software engineer for several IT infrastructure and technology servicing companies.

He collaborated with the Outernet (free data, forever) project as a volunteer hardware and software tester for Lighthouse and Raspberry Pi-based DIY Outernet receivers based on Ku band satellite frequencies. Pradeeka is the author of *Building Arduino PLCs, Internet of Things with Arduino Blueprints, IoT: Building Arduino-Based Projects,* and *Raspberry Pi 3 Projects for Java Programmers.*

About the Technical Reviewer

Michael Rimicans has been tinkering with the micro:bit since its release and has enjoyed making cool things. He is also a STEM ambassador and CodeClub volunteer. He can normally be found at @heeedt on Twitter.

Foreword

How can educators and education systems prepare children for an uncertain future job market?

That's the challenge that the BBC chose to take on, back in 2012.

In the UK the BBC not only produces great TV and radio content, the BBC Learning department also plays an important role in providing curricula linked educational content and support for UK school children and learners of all ages. The introduction of the BBC micro computer in the 80s had a profound and transformational impact on the IT sector in the UK that is still felt to this day, and the BBC saw that an updated initiative could have a similarly transformational impact for the current generation of young learners.

A bold and ambitious plan was drawn up and the BBC micro:bit project was born!

This project culminated in 2016 when the BBC and a partnership of 30 organisations (including ARM, Samsung and Microsoft) distributed 1 million BBC micro:bit mini computers into high schools in the UK. Then in October 2016 the Micro:bit Educational Foundation was formed to take on micro:bit and bring it to a global audience. The coding revolution had begun!

The BBC micro:bit is a small programmable device. Its a mixture between a very small computer and a programmable embedded board. It is easy to program, very versatile, and designed with young learners in mind. In particular it is designed to be easy to get started with for people who have never programmed before.

The success of BBC micro:bit in the UK (and a fast growing number of other countries around the world) is not just down to the innovative hardware device though. It's the micro:bit ecosystem that makes micro:bit such a great tool for educators, children and anyone interested in using tech in inventive and fun ways! Our ecosystem consists of the hardware, a thriving market for peripherals and add ones, an ever growing library of great books (including this one) and our great code editors. There is also over 1000 amazing projects, lessons and fun ideas that are freely available online as well as vibrant communities of enthusiasts. The Micro:bit Educational Foundation is here to support and develop the ecosystem.

But the most important component of our ecosystem are the people that use it.

So, thank you for picking up this book. We at the Micro:bit Educational Foundation wish you good luck on your micro:bit journey!

Sincerely

—The Micro:bit Educational Foundation

Please note that this book is not an official or certified publication of the Micro:bit Educational Foundation.

CHAPTER 1

Getting Ready

Welcome to the exciting world of building projects with BBC micro:bit!
First, this chapter introduces the micro:bit and provides a shopping guide
for micro:bit and its accessories, including starter kits and inventor's
kits. Then you will learn how to power the micro:bit board using various
powering options. The most interesting part of this chapter is when you
write your first code for the micro:bit with the online Python editor, and
the Mu editor. You will also learn how to flash a program to the micro:bit
and run it. The latter part of the chapter introduces working with REPL
(Read-Evaluate-Print-Loop) using the Mu editor to run code line-by-line
without flashing the complete program to the micro:bit.

What Is the BBC micro:bit?

The micro:bit (see Figure 1-1) is a pocket-sized microcontroller board
designed by the BBC for use in computer education in the UK. It is part
of the BBC's "Make It Digital" campaign (see `http://www.bbc.co.uk/
makeitdigital`) and is becoming increasingly popular with people around
the world.

© Pradeeka Seneviratne 2018
P. Seneviratne, *Beginning BBC micro:bit*, https://doi.org/10.1007/978-1-4842-3360-3_1

Figure 1-1. *The BBC micro:bit in use (image courtesy of the micro:bit Foundation)*

It is the successor of the BBC micro (see Figure 1-2), which was introduced in 1980s. You can read more about the BBC micro by visiting https://en.wikipedia.org/wiki/BBC_Micro.

Figure 1-2. *BBC micro from the 1980s (source:* `https://en.wikipedia.org/wiki/BBC_Micro`*)*

What's on the micro:bit?

Before you start coding with the micro:bit, you should familiarize yourself with the key features of the board.

Figure 1-3 shows the front of the micro:bit board. The board has one of four color schemes, and you don't know which color you will get when purchasing a board.

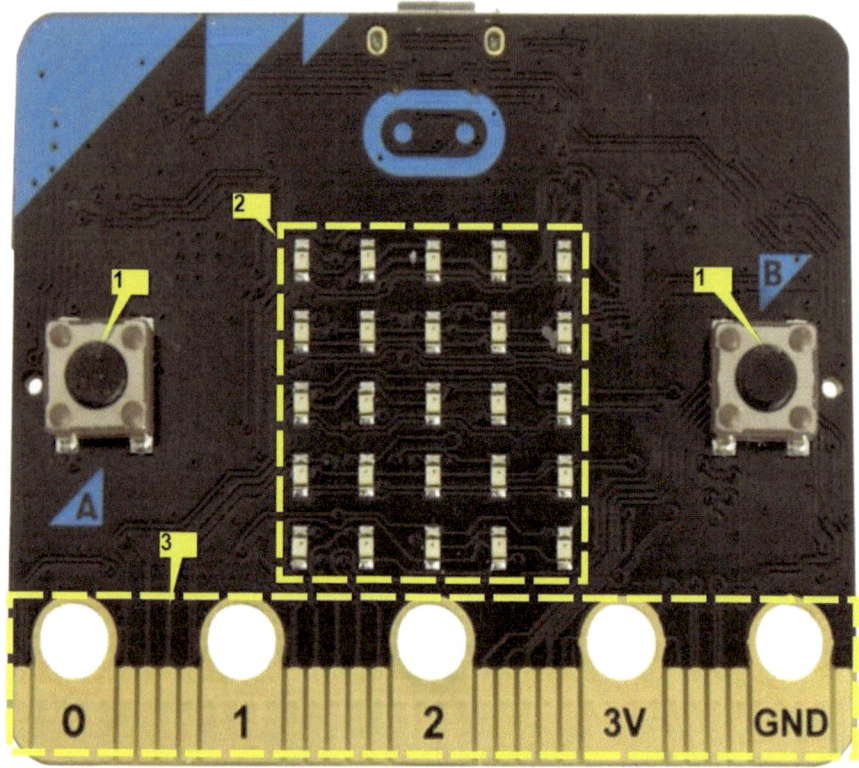

Figure 1-3. *Front view of the micro:bit board (image courtesy of Kitronik)*

The front of the micro:bit board is designed to interact with the user by exposing the following components, as labeled on Figure 1-3:

1. *The buttons*: There are two momentary pushbuttons labeled A and B that allow you to directly interact with your programs. You can configure them to control a game or pause and skip songs on a playlist, for example.

2. *Display*: The display consists of 25 surface-mounted red LEDs arranged as a 5x5 grid that allow you to display text, images, and animations. The display can be used as an ambient light sensor too.

3. *Edge connector*: The total of 25 pins on the edge connector allow you to connect various sensors and actuators, access I/O lines, and connect to power and ground. They include an LED matrix, two pushbuttons, an I2C bus, and a SPI. The 0, 1, 2, 3V, and GND pins are exposed as ring connectors, which allow you to easily connect crocodile or banana clips. The 0, 1, and 2 pins are specialized for capacitive sensing. All the pins can be accessed with the Kitronik edge connector breakout board (see Figure 1-4) or the SparkFun micro:bit breakout board (see Figure 1-5).

Figure 1-4. *Kitronik edge connector breakout board (image courtesy of Kitronik:* `https://www.kitronik.co.uk/5601b-edge-connector-breakout-board-for-bbc-microbit-pre-built.html`*)*

Figure 1-5. *SparkFun micro:bit breakout (image courtesy of SparkFun Electronics:* `https://www.sparkfun.com/ products/13989`*)*

Figure 1-6 shows the pinout of the micro:bit edge connector. You will learn in detail about the micro:bit edge connector and how to work with it in Chapter 4, "Using Inputs and Outputs".

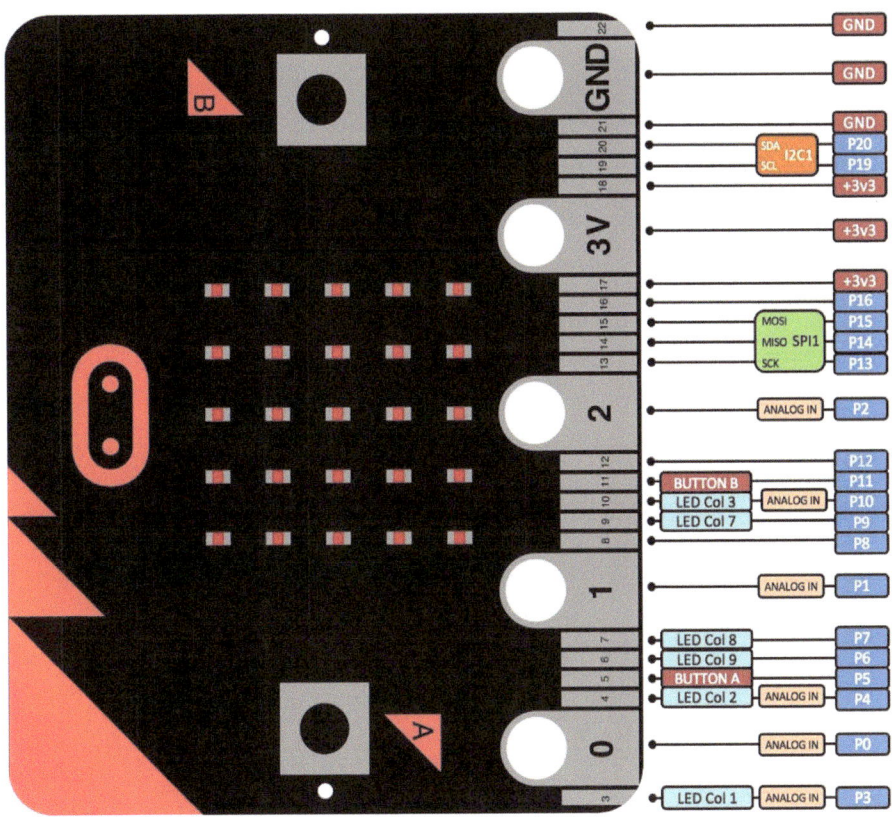

Figure 1-6. *The micro:bit pinout (image courtesy of micro:bit Foundation)*

The back of the board (see Figure 1-7) consists of a host of electronic components and hardware.

Figure 1-7. *Back view of the micro:bit board (image courtesy of Kitronik)*

The following list explains the most important things that can be found on the back of the board, as numbered in Figure 1-7:

1. *Processor (Nordic nRF51822)*: 16MHz 32-bit ARM
    Cortex-M0 CPU, 256KB flash memory, 16KB Static
    RAM (https://developer.arm.com/products/
    processors/cortex-m/cortex-m0), with 2.4GHz
    Bluetooth low energy wireless networking, which
    allows you to pair the micro:bit with Bluetooth
    enabled mobile devices running Android and iOS.

2. *Compass (NXP/Freescale MAG3110)*: Allows you to measure magnetic field strength in each of three axes.

3. *Accelerometer (NXP/Freescale MMA8652)*: Allows you to measure the acceleration and movement along three axes.

4. *USB controller (NXP/Freescale KL26Z)*: 48MHz ARM Cortex-M0+ core microcontroller, which includes a full-speed USB 2.0 On-The-Go (OTG) controller, used as a communication interface between the USB and the main Nordic microcontroller.

5. *Micro USB connector*: Allows you to connect the micro:bit board with a computer for flashing codes or power it with 5V USB power.

6. *Bluetooth smart antenna*: A printed antenna that transmits Bluetooth signals in the 2.4GHz band.

7. RESET button: Allows you to reset the micro:bit and restart the currently running program or bring the micro:bit into maintenance mode.

8. *Battery connector/socket*: Allows you to power the micro:bit board with 2 AAA batteries.

9. *System LED*: The yellow color LED indicates USB power (solid) and data transfer (flashing). It doesn't indicate the battery power.

10. *Edge connector*: Includes 21 pins

Buying a micro:bit

A single micro:bit board (see Figure 1-8) is more than enough to build most of the applications that you can imagine, but if you're planning to build the peer-to-peer and radio networks that we will be discussing in this book, you need at least two micro:bit boards.

Figure 1-8. *micro:bit board only*

You can buy micro:bit boards from various local and online sellers. Table 1-1 shows a list of online sellers that typically stock the micro:bit along with the product name and product page. These sellers usually ship the micro:bit to any country in the world. However, contact the seller before ordering to verify if there are any shipping restrictions to your country.

Table 1-1. *Where to Buy the micro:bit*

Vendor	Product Name	Product Page
Kitronik	BBC micro:bit (board only)	`https://www.kitronik.co.uk/5613-bbc-microbit-board-only.html`
	BBC micro:bit (board only), retail pack	`https://www.kitronik.co.uk/5614-bbc-microbit-board-only-retail-pack.html`
SparkFun Electronics	micro:bit board	`https://www.sparkfun.com/products/14208`
Adafruit Industries	BBC micro:bit	`https://www.adafruit.com/product/3530`
Pimoroni	micro:bit only	`https://shop.pimoroni.com/products/microbit`
Seeed Studios	micro:bit	`https://www.seeedstudio.com/Micro%3ABit-p-2886.html`

Buying a Starter Kit

Starter kits usually provide everything you need to connect the micro:bit to your computer and power it with batteries. A starter kit typically includes following parts:

- The micro:bit

- A micro USB cable

- Battery holder

- Two AAA batteries (optional)

Table 1-2 shows a list of online sellers that offer starter kits at competitive prices.

Table 1-2. *Where to Buy the Starter Kits*

Vendor	Product Page
Kitronik	`https://www.kitronik.co.uk/5615-bbc-microbit-starter-kit.html`
PiHut	`https://thepihut.com/products/micro-bit-starter-kit`
Pi Supply	`https://www.pi-supply.com/product/microbit-go/`

Figure 1-9 shows the BBC micro:bit starter kit by Kitronik (`https://www.kitronik.co.uk`).

Figure 1-9. *BBC micro:bit Starter Kit by Kitronik: (a) micro:bit (b) micro USB cable (c) battery holder (d) two AAA batteries. Image courtesy of Kitronik (`https://www.kitronik.co.uk`)*

Buying an Inventor's Kit

Inventor's kits provide a host of things you need to start building most of the basic to advanced projects in the micro:bit. Table 1-3 shows some of the inventor's kits that were available at the time of this writing.

Table 1-3. *Where to Buy Inventor's Kits*

Vendor	Product Name	Product Page
Kitronik	Inventor's kit for the BBC micro:bit	`https://www.kitronik.co.uk/5603-inventors-kit-for-the-bbc-microbit.html`
	BBC micro:bit with inventor's kit and accessories	`https://www.kitronik.co.uk/5618-bbc-microbit-with-inventors-kit-and-accessories.html`
SparkFun Electronics	SparkFun inventor's kit for micro:bit	`https://www.sparkfun.com/products/14300`
Seeed Studio	Grove inventor kit for micro:bit	`https://www.seeedstudio.com/Grove-Inventor-Kit-for-micro%3Abit-p-2891.html`

Figure 1-10 shows the Kitronik inventor's kit for the BBC micro:bit. The kit includes the following components.

- Perspex mounting plate

- Potentiometer and finger adjust spindle

- Plastic spacers 10mm (2)

- Sticky fixer for battery pack

- Small prototype breadboard

- Terminal connector

- Push switches (4)

- Motor

- Transistor

- Red 5mm LEDs (2)

- Orange 5mm LEDs (2)

- Yellow 5mm LEDs (2)

- Green 5mm LEDs (2)

- RGB 5mm LED

- Fan blade

- 2.2KΩ resistors (5)

- 10KΩ resistors (5)

- 47Ω resistors (5)

- Edge connector breakout board for BBC micro:bit

- Miniature LDR

- Male to male jumper wires (10)

- Male to female jumper wires (10)

- Self-adhesive rubber feet (4)

- 470uF electrolytic capacitor

- Piezo element buzzer

- Pan head M3 machine screw (4)

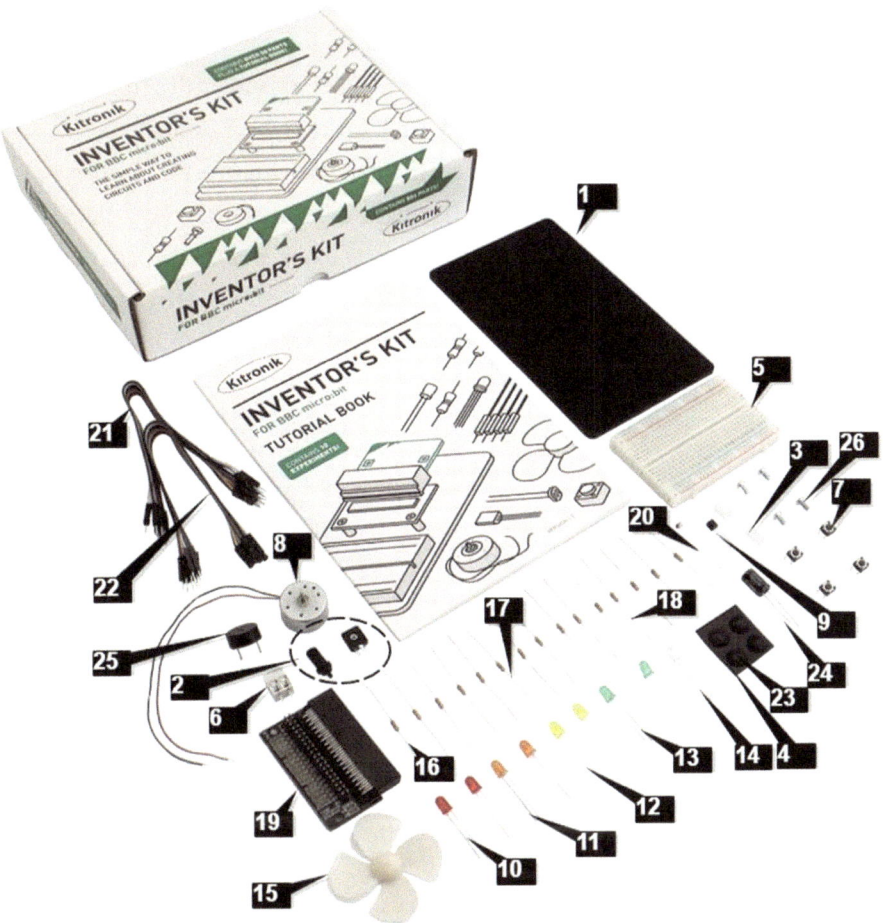

Figure 1-10. *Kitronik inventor's kit for the BBC micro:bit (image courtesy of Kitronik)*

micro:bit Accessories

If you don't have a micro:bit starter kit or an inventor's kit, you should prepare the following accessories and connect the micro:bit to a computer and then use the micro:bit with battery power.

15

Batteries and Battery Holders

You need two Zinc Carbon or Alkaline batteries to power the micro:bit. Kitronik stocks a good quality battery case for two AAA batteries.

The AAA battery cage with JST connector (see Figure 1-11) from Kitronik has color-coded power leads and a JST connector. You can purchase a battery holder by visiting `https://www.kitronik.co.uk/2271-2xaaa-battery-cage-with-jst-connector.html`. If you are planning to build the peer-to-peer and radio networks with micro:bit that we discuss in Chapter 9, you should purchase two battery holders.

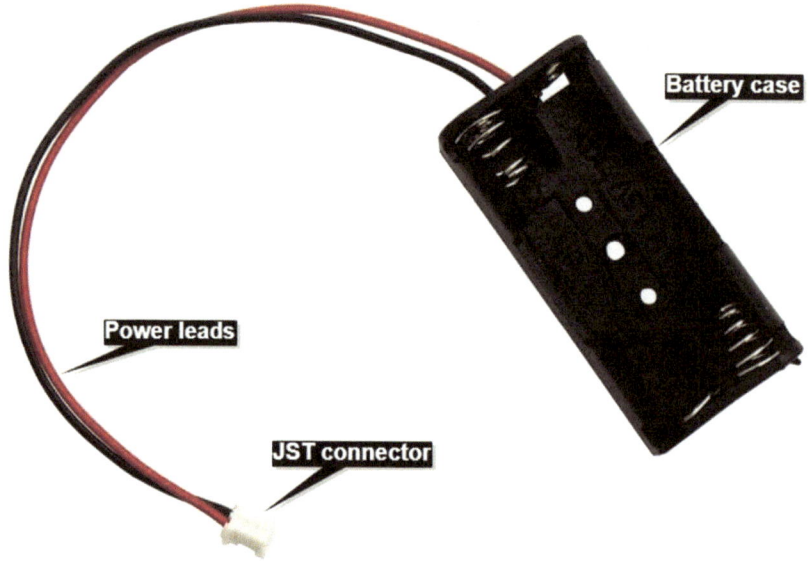

Figure 1-11. *AAA battery cage with JST connector (image courtesy of Kitronik)*

USB Cable

You need a Type-A to Micro-B USB cable (see Figure 1-12) to connect the micro:bit to a computer. This is the same cable usually bundled with many mobile phones and some consumer products. You can purchase a 1m USB Type-A to Micro-B USB Noodle Cable at `https://www.kitronik.co.uk/4154-1m-usb-type-a-to-micro-b-usb-noodle-cable.html`.

Figure 1-12. *Type-A to Micro-B USB cable (image courtesy of Kitronik)*

Crocodile Clips

You will need a few crocodile clips (see Figure 1-13) to build prototypes without soldering wires with ring connectors of the edge connector. It is not wise to use crocodile clips with small connectors. The wire can be secured with the two side notches located at the back of the clip.

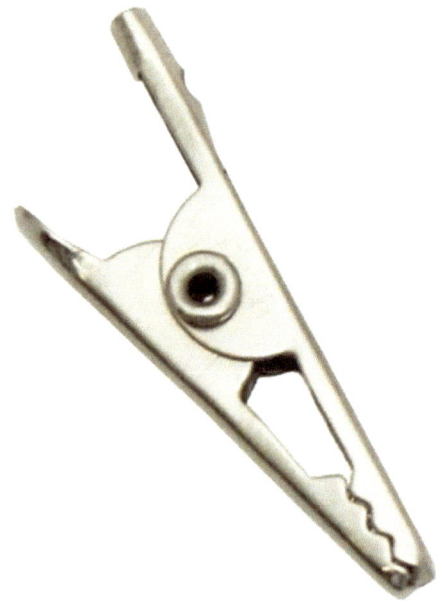

Figure 1-13. A crocodile clip (image courtesy of Kitronik: https://www.kitronik.co.uk/2470-28mm-crocodile-clips-pack-of-50.html)

Powering Your micro:bit

The micro:bit is powered by 3.3v. This can be provided by suitable batteries connected via the battery connector or via the USB connector. The USB controller chip will automatically convert the 5v to 3.3v. It can also be powered via the 3v pad on the edge connector but this may not be suitable for beginners.

Note   The micro:bit can also be powered via the 3v pad on the edge connector, but this may not be suitable for beginners.

Powering the micro:bit with Batteries

Powering the micro:bit with two AAA batteries is the easiest way to get started and to see how it works. You need the following components to power the micro:bit with batteries:

- Two AAA Zinc Carbon or Alkaline batteries (use the same types of batteries without mixing them)

- AAA battery case with a wire and clip

Follow these steps to power the micro:bit with batteries:

1. First, insert the two batteries into the battery case in the correct orientation. Then, connect the JST connector of the battery case to the battery connector of the micro:bit firmly without forcing it (see Figure 1-14). The JST connector will only connect one way with the battery connector.

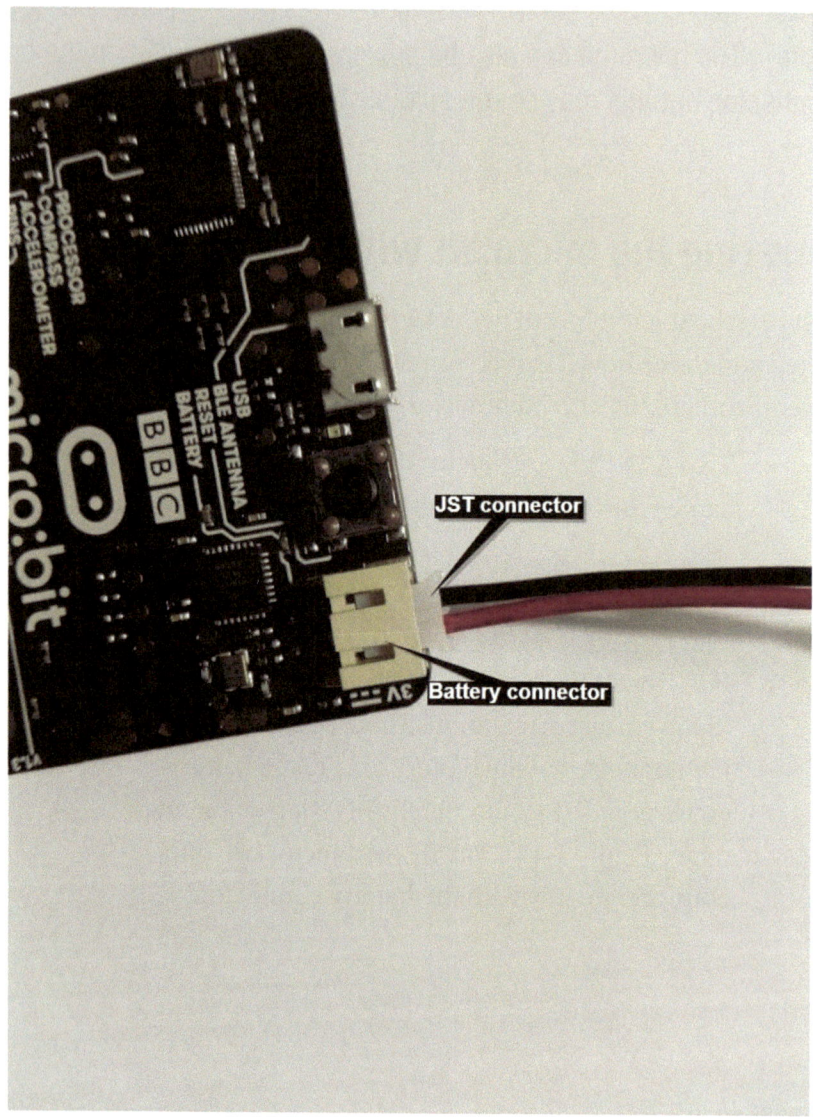

Figure 1-14. *Connecting JST connector to battery connector*

2. When you power the micro:bit the very first time, a
    pre-loaded demo program will automatically run
    on the micro:bit. This program will show you how
    to use the screen for displaying text and images,
    use the two built-in buttons, interact with the
    accelerometer, and play games.

Note   When you flash a new program to the micro:bit, the demo
program is erased. However, you can flash it again by downloading
the demo program at `https://support.microbit.org/`
`helpdesk/attachments/19002943122` or from the source code
archive of this book (visit source codes ➤ chapter1 ➤ BBC-MicroBit-
First-Experience-1460979530935.hex).

Powering micro:bit with a USB

You need one of the following components to power the micro:bit with
USB power:

- Computer

- USB battery pack

- USB power adapter

Follow these steps to power the micro:bit with USB power using a
computer:

1. Connect the Micro-B connecter of the USB cable to
    the Micro-B socket of the micro:bit (see Figure 1-15).

Figure 1-15. *Connecting the Micro-B connector to the Micro-B socket*

2. Then, connect the Type-A connector of the USB cable to the USB port of your computer (see Figure 1-16).

Figure 1-16. *Connecting the Type-A connector to a USB port (image courtesy of Micro:bit Foundation)*

3. The system LED (see Figure 1-17) on the back of the micro:bit will light up in yellow. This indicates the presence of USB power.

Figure 1-17. *System LED indicates the presence of USB power (image courtesy of Kitronik)*

Alternative Ways to Power the micro:bit

The micro:bit can be powered with some specially designed power sources as well. For example, the MI:power board can supply 3V through the 3V pin of the micro:bit board and the Seenov solar battery can supply 5V through the micro USB port of the micro:bit board.

MI:power Board

The MI:power board (see Figure 1-18) allows you to build compact prototypes without using a bulky battery holder. This is great when you are building wearable, portable, and handheld devices with micro:bit because it uses the same footprint of the micro:bit, and it is lightweight of course. It has a 3V coin cell, a power on/off switch, and an integrated buzzer that helps you use it as an audio output. You can read more technical information about the MI:power board by visiting `https://www.kitronik.co.uk/5610-mipower-board-for-the-bbc-microbit.html`.

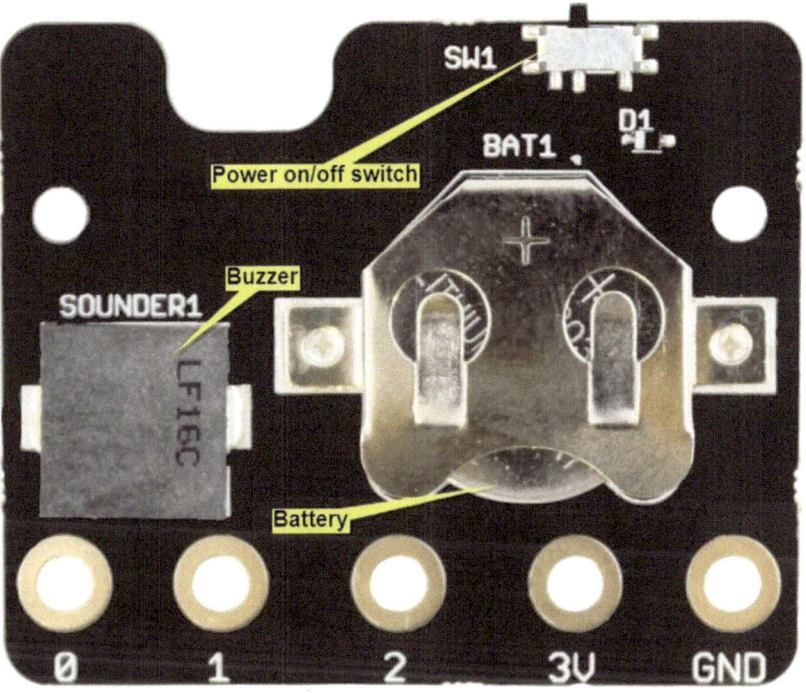

Figure 1-18. *MI:power board (image courtesy of Kitronik)*

Seenov Solar Battery

The Seenov solar battery (see Figure 1-19) is an ideal solution to power your micro:bit with solar power. Once you have completely charged the solar battery with a solar panel or USB, it can power the micro:bit for five days or more. The charger board can be purchased with or without the solar panel of your choice. Here are the product links.

- Charger board only: `https://www.seenov.com/product/11/`

- Charger board with solar panels: `https://www.seenov.com/product/solar-battery-bbc-microbit-wo-solar-panel/`

Figure 1-19. *Seenov Solar Battery (image courtesy of Seenov)*

Powered through the 3v Pin

The micro:bit can be powered through the 3v pin on the edge connector. You should apply a suitable protection, like a voltage regulator, to protect the micro:bit.

For example, you can use a 3.7v LiPo battery to power the micro:bit through a 3.3v voltage regulator. The MCP1702 can output regulated 3.3v with an input voltage range from 2.7V to 13.2V. Here is a list of all the parts needed to build the circuit.

- 3.7v LiPo battery (`https://www.sparkfun.com/products/13813`)

- MCP1702-3302E/TO voltage regulator (`http://uk.farnell.com/microchip/mcp1702-3302e-to/ic-v-reg-ldo-250ma-to-92-3/dp/1331485`)

- 1uF ceramic capacitors (2)

Figure 1-20 shows the circuit and Figure 1-21 shows the wiring diagram for the power supply.

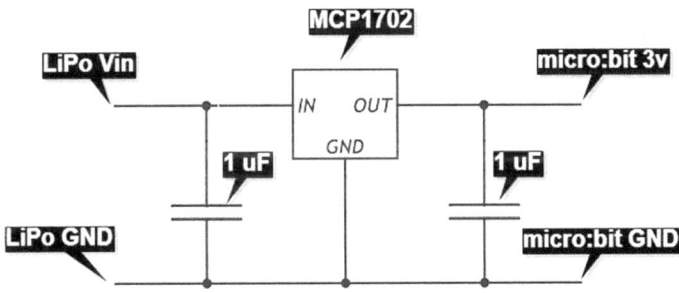

Figure 1-20. *3.3v regulator circuit with MCP1702 voltage regulator*

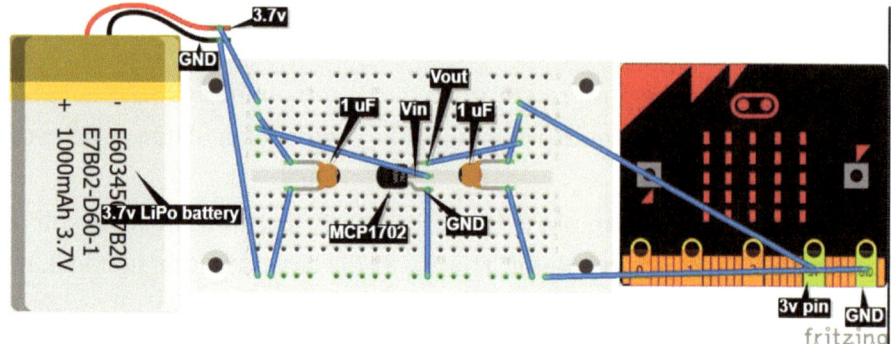

Figure 1-21. *Wiring diagram for MCP1702 3.3v voltage regulator*

Creating Your First Program with Online Python Editor

The version of Python that runs on the BBC micro:bit is called MicroPython. It is designed to run on small microcontroller boards like micro:bit.

Coding with the Online Python Editor

You can use the online Python editor hosted at http://python.microbit.org/editor.html to write MicroPython code for micro:bit and get the binary file of the code for flashing. Here is what you will need to write to execute the MicroPython program.

- A micro:bit

- USB Type-A to Micro-B cable

- Any modern computer with a USB port and an up to date browser

- An Internet connection

The following steps guide you on how to write your first program for microbit with the online Python editor.

1. Connect the microbit to your computer using a USB cable.

2. Open your favorite web browser and access the online Python editor at `http://python.microbit.org/editor.html#` (see Figure 1-22).

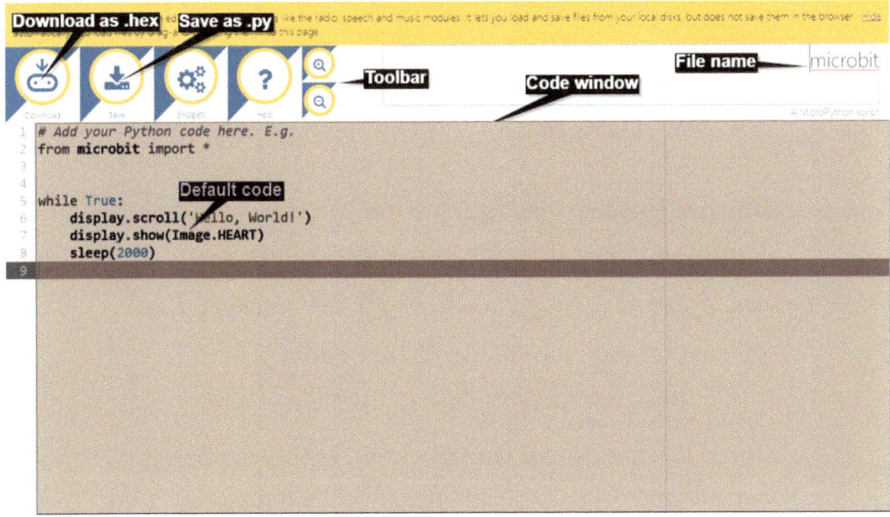

Figure 1-22. *Online Python editor*

3. Delete the default program's lines and type the program into the editor, as shown in Listing 1-1.

Listing 1-1. Displaying and scrolling text

```
from microbit import *

display.scroll("Hello World!", delay=150, loop=True)
```

4. Figure 1-23 shows the code window.

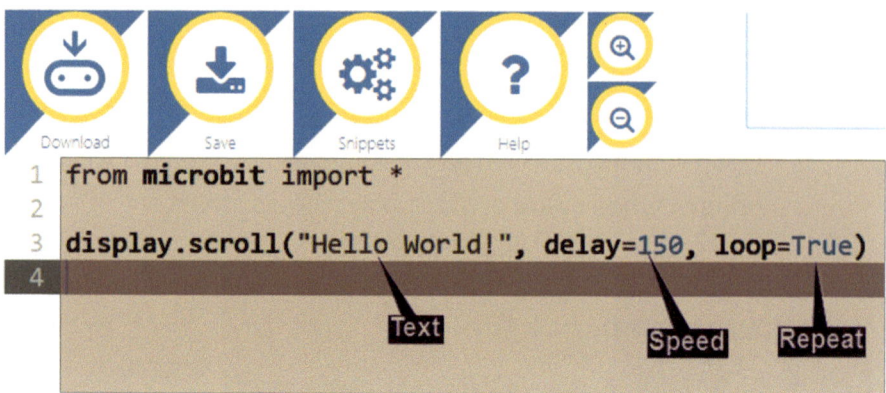

Figure 1-23. *The 'Hello World' code on the code editor*

5. The first line loads all the code required to allow you to program the micro:bit with MicroPython.

6. The `display.scroll()` command tells MicroPython to use the scroll part of the display command to scroll the message provided on the LED display.

7. The delay parameter controls how fast the text is scrolling. `delay=150` tells MicroPython to use 150 milliseconds (0.15 seconds) to control the speed of scrolling. (Recall that 1000 milliseconds is 1 second.)

8. `loop=True` tells MicroPython to repeat the animation forever.

9. Type the file name Listing 1-1 in the Filename box and click the Save button to save the Python source code to your computer as a .py file (see Figure 1-24). By default, the source code file will download and save on your computer's Downloads folder. The editor will automatically replace any spaces in the file name with underscores. Therefore, you will get a file named Listing_1-1.py.

Figure 1-24. *Saving the python source file (.py)*

10. Click the Download button to download the Listing_1-1.hex file of your code, which is a binary file to your computer (see Figure 1-25). For Windows and the Mac, the default download location is the `Downloads` folder.

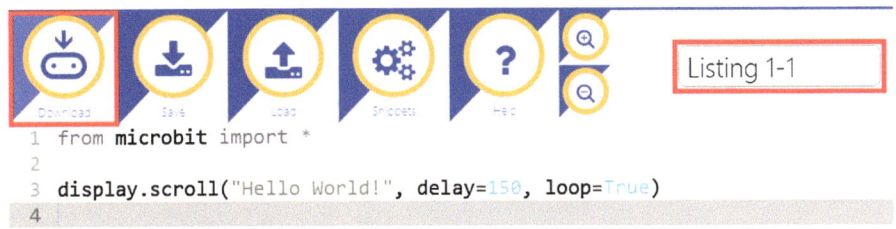

Figure 1-25. *Downloading/saving the binary file (.hex)*

11. When you connect the micro:bit to a Windows or Mac, the computer recognizes the internal storage of the micro:bit as a removable disk and it appears as `MICROBIT`. If you are using Windows, the micro:bit drive can be found under Devices and Drives and for the Mac, it can be found under Devices.

Note Notice that the capacity of the micro:bit drive is about 8MB and the file system is FAT. As a best practice, eject the drive from the operating system before unplugging it from the computer.

12. Drag and drop (or copy and paste) the downloaded Listing_1-1.hex file from the Downloads folder to the micro:bit drive (see Figure 1-26). The LED on the back of your micro:bit flashes during the transfer, which only takes a few seconds. Once the flashing stops, your code is uploaded.

Note It may also be worth noting that the browser may ask you where to save the .hex file. If it does, save the file directly onto the micro:bit.

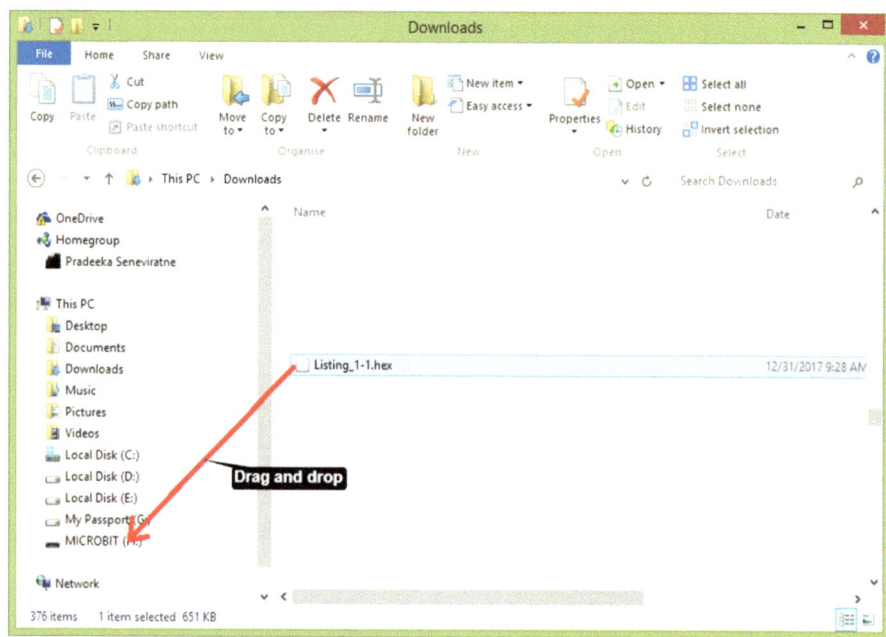

Figure 1-26. *Copying a .hex file to the micro:bit*

> **Note**   Once your .hex file has been used to program the micro:bit, it will be removed automatically from the drive.

13. The program automatically starts once the copy operation is completed. If your program doesn't start after flashing the .hex file, press the RESET button to start it.

> **Note**   When the yellow LED stops flashing, the micro:bit will restart and your code will run. If there is an error, you will see a helpful message scroll across the device's display.

Coding with Mu

Mu is one of the easiest Python editors you can use to write MicroPython programs for micro:bit. It is a cross-platform editor that works on Windows, OSX, Linux, and Raspberry Pi. The main advantage of Mu is that it includes REPL, which allows you to run codes line by line without flashing the complete program to the micro:bit.

The Mu editor can be downloaded at `https://codewith.mu/` for Windows, OSX, Linux, and Raspberry Pi. For Windows, you get an executable file that can run directly without being installed on the operating system. At the time of this writing, the latest version of Mu for Windows was 0.9.13. You can also directly download it from `https://github.com/mu-editor/mu/releases/download/v0.9.13/ mu-0.9.13.win.exe`.

When you run the downloaded Mu executable file (`mu-x.x.xx.win.exe`), you will get the Mu code editor shown in Figure 1-27.

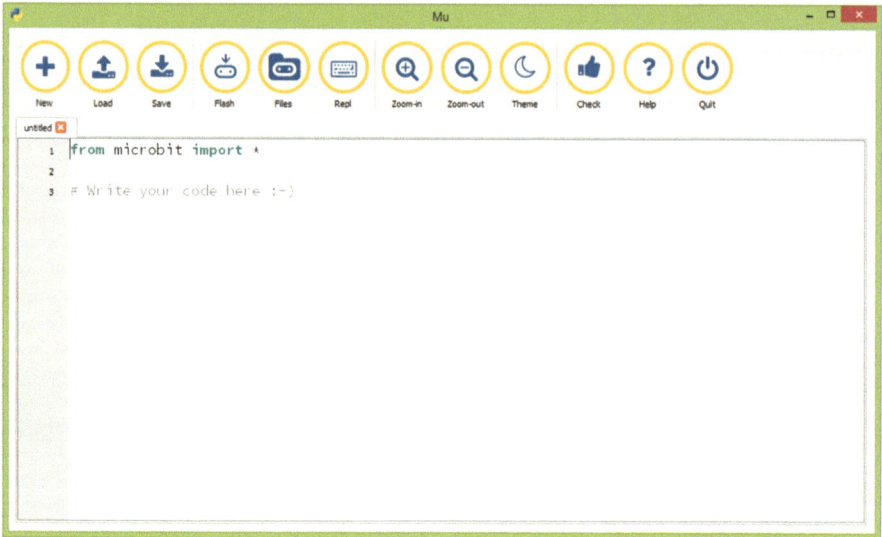

Figure 1-27. _Mu code editor_

1. Write the MicroPython code shown in Listing 1-2 using the Mu editor.

Listing 1-2. Displaying and scrolling text

```
from microbit import *

display.scroll("Hello World!", delay=150, loop=True)
```

2. Once you have done this, you can save the MicroPython source code as a .py file to the computer using the Save button in the toolbar (see Figure 1-28).

Figure 1-28. *The Save button*

3. You can also directly flash the binary (the .hex file)
    to the micro:bit using the Flash button in the toolbar
    (see Figure 1-29).

Figure 1-29. *The Flash button*

4. The Check button can be used to check the code
    for errors before flashing it to the micro:bit (see
    Figure 1-30).

Figure 1-30. *The Check button*

Using REPL with Mu

As mentioned, you can use Mu to run code line by line without flashing the complete program to the micro:bit. This is known as REPL (Read-Evaluate-Print-Loop).

For the REPL to work with Windows, you should install the mbed Windows serial port driver. The driver can be downloaded from `https://developer.mbed.org/handbook/Windows-serial-configuration`.

Run the code listed in Listing 1-3 with REPL.

Listing 1-3. Using REPL to execute code on micro:bit

```
from microbit import *

display.scroll("Hello from Mu REPL", delay=150, loop=True)
```

1. Before using the REPL interface, an empty MicroPython code must be flashed onto the microbit. This can be done by first clicking the New button followed by the Flash button on the toolbar.

2. Then click the Repl button on the toolbar to open an interactive shell (see Figure 1-31).

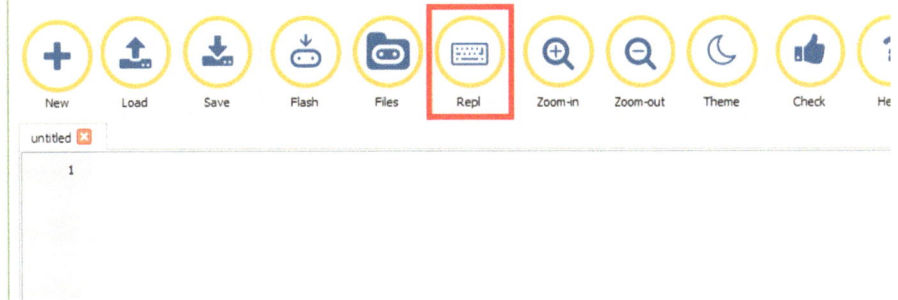

Figure 1-31. *The Repl button*

3. Type the first line of the program, `from microbit import *`, and press Enter (see Figure 1-32).

Figure 1-32. *Writing on the interactive shell*

4. Then type the second line, `display.scroll("Hello from Mu REPL", delay=150, loop=True)`, and press Enter again (see Figure 1-33).

Figure 1-33. *Writing on the interactive shell*

5. The Hello from Mu REPL text will continually scroll across the micro:bit LED screen.

Summary

Now you know how to set up your development environment with micro:bit and code your micro:bit with online Python editor and the Mu Editor. You also learned how to use REPL with the Mu editor to run MicroPython code line-by-line without flashing the complete program to the micro:bit.

The next chapter introduces how to display images and build animations on the micro:bit display.

CHAPTER 2

Working with Display and Images

By now, you should be fairly comfortable with the basics of micro:bit. You've learned how to set up the development environment and write simple code with the online Python editor and the Mu editor.

In this chapter, you learn about the micro:bit built-in LED screen. You'll see how to turn LEDs on and off in the micro:bit display and control the brightness of the LEDs. Then you'll learn how to turn the LED screen on and off in order to use the GPIO pins associated with the LED screen. After that, you learn how to display the built-in images and image lists and create your own images and image lists. Finally, you'll see how to create animations with built-in image lists and your own image lists.

The micro:bit Built-In LED Display

micro:bit is great for building things that need a visual output. You can do this by using the built-in LED display on the front of the board. The built-in display consists of 25 red LEDs arranged as a 5x5 grid. You can display text, images, and animations with these 25 LEDs, thereby making your project more interactive and providing a richer user experience.

© Pradeeka Seneviratne 2018
P. Seneviratne, *Beginning BBC micro:bit*, https://doi.org/10.1007/978-1-4842-3360-3_2

You can use the x and y coordinates to specify the location of a LED in the grid. Figure 2-1 shows the column and row numbers associated with the LED grid. You can read the column numbers (0 to 5) along the x axis and the row numbers (0 to 5) along the y axis.

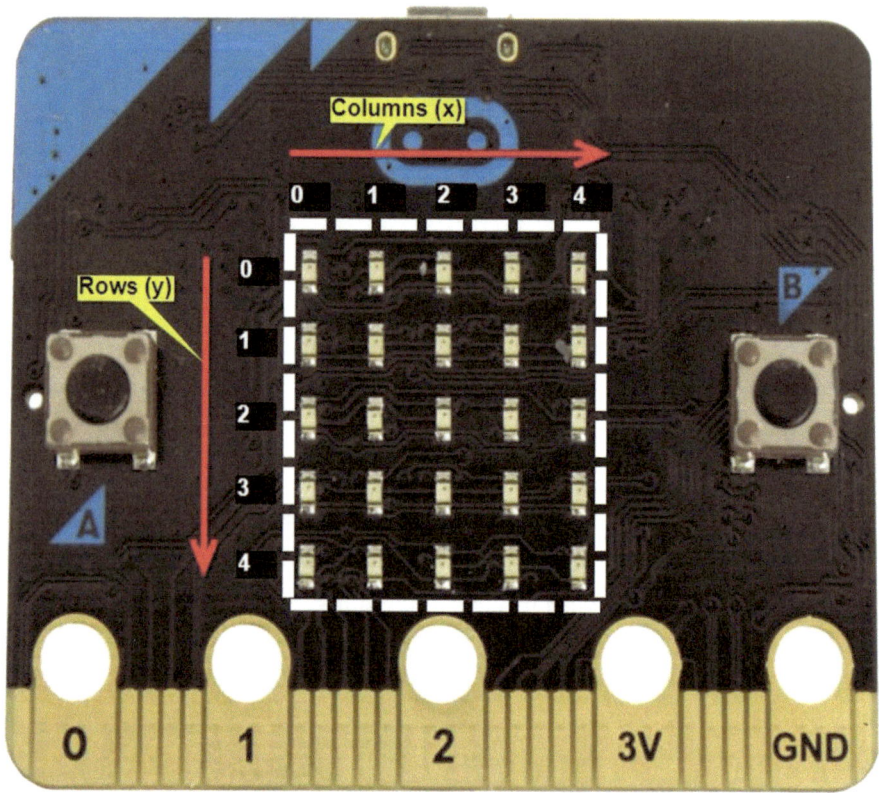

Figure 2-1. *Built-in LED display consists of columns and rows*

The address of a LED can be written using the associated column and row number. When creating code, you start your counts at 0, hence five LEDs will be addressed as 0, 1, 2, 3, and 4. As an example, Figure 2-2 shows an LED on the display located at the address **(3, 2),** where 3 is the column number and 2 is the row number.

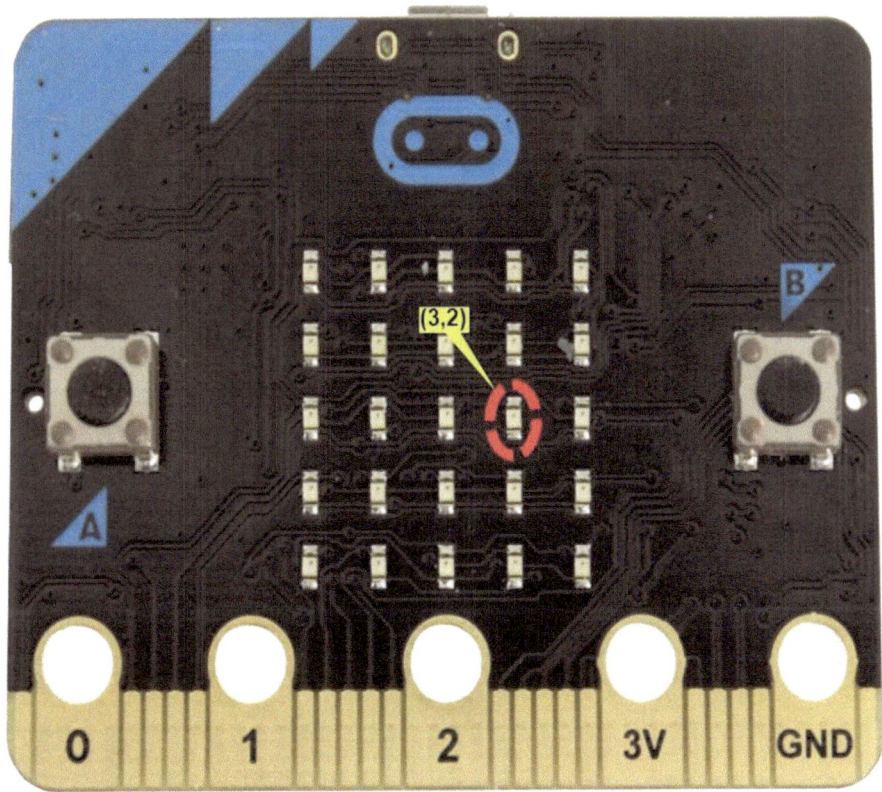

Figure 2-2. *LED located at the address column 3 and row 2 (3, 2)*

Turning LEDs On and Off

This section starts with a simple example and shows you how to turn an LED on and off in the LED screen. The code shown in Listing 2-1 blinks the LED located in address (3,2).

Listing 2-1. Turning an LED On and Off

```
from microbit import *

while True:
    display.set_pixel(3, 2, 9) # turn on the LED
    sleep(1000) # wait for 1 second
    display.set_pixel(3, 2, 0) # turn off the LED
    sleep(1000) # wait for 1 second
```

The while True statement helps you iterate the block of statements underneath it as an infinite loop. The display.set_pixel() function allows you to tell the MicroPython where the LED is located in the LED screen, using **x** and **y**. The first parameter takes the column number and the second parameter takes the row number. The third parameter is set to 9 to turn on the LED and 0 to turn off the LED. You will learn about the third parameter of the display.set_pixel() function in the next section. The MicroPython code will turn on the LED for one second and turn off the LED for one second. This sequence will continue and you can see a blinking effect.

Note   Python uses indentation to mark blocks of code. You should indent each line of the block by the same amount. You can use the Tab key on your keyboard to insert the same amount of indentation.

```
while True:
[TAB]display.set_pixel(3, 2, 9)
...
```

Setting and Getting the Brightness of an LED

Controlling the brightness of an image is a key factor of graphics and multimedia. In micro:bit, you can set or get the brightness level of any LED in the grid. This is done through the third parameter of the `display.set_pixel()` function.

Setting Brightness

The third parameter of the `display.set_pixel()` function accepts a brightness level for the LED between 0-9, where 0 indicates minimum brightness (LED is off) and 9 indicates maximum brightness.

Listing 2-2 shows the code that sets the brightness level of the LED located in column 3 and row 2 to 5.

Listing 2-2. Setting LED Brightness

```
from microbit import *

display.set_pixel(3,2,5) # set the brightness level to 5
```

Getting Brightness

The **display.get_pixel()** function, on the other hand, *returns* the brightness level of a given LED. Listing 2-3 shows the code that gets the brightness level of the LED located in column 3 and row 2.

Listing 2-3. Getting LED Brightness

```
from microbit import *

display.set_pixel(3,2,5) # first set the brightness level to 5
pixel_brightness = display.get_pixel(3,2) # then get the
current brightness level
display.scroll("brightness is: "+str(pixel_brightness))
```

The micro:bit display will show the following output:

```
Brightness is: 5
```

Clearing the Display

The display.clear() function allows you to set the brightness level of all LEDs to 0. This is helpful when you want to turn off all the LEDs at once and clear the display.

Listing 2-4 shows the code used to clear the display, wait a few seconds, and then turn on the display to full brightness.

Listing 2-4. Clearing the LED Display

```
from microbit import *

display.show('X')
sleep(5000) #wait for 5 seconds
display.clear() # set the brightness level of all the LEDs to 0
sleep(2000) #wait for 2 seconds
for x in range(0, 5):
    for y in range(0, 5):
        sleep(100) # slow down the code long enough for the
        user to see the LEDs turn on and off in sequence
        display.set_pixel(x,y,9) # then set the brightness
        level of all the LEDs to 9 using for loop
```

The for command can be used to create a loop, which will then run the required code n amount of times.

The first for command will create a loop and run the code five times. The number of times can be defined with the range() function. The second for command, which resides inside the first for command, will create another loop and execute the display.set_pixel() function five times to turn on the LEDs. Brightness level 9 is used to turn on LEDs at full brightness. So, these two `for` loops will execute the `display.set_pixel()` function 25 times for each LED.

Figure 2-3 shows the sequence of executing the two loops.

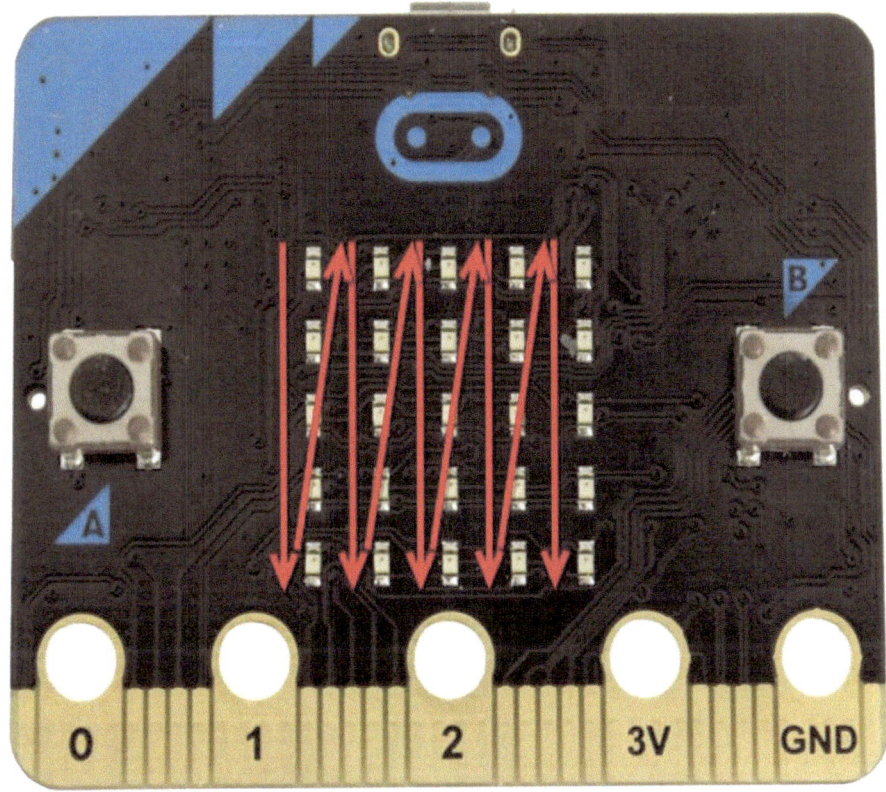

Figure 2-3. *Execution of two for loops: x and y*

Turning the Display On and Off

The `display.off()` function turns off the display and allows you to use the GPIO pins (3, 4, 6, 7, 9, and 10) associated with the display for other purposes. As you can see in Figure 2-4, some of the GPIO pins are connected to the LED display's rows and/or columns, so if you want to use them, you have to switch the display off. Otherwise, it will keep switching the pins, and you will see unexpected display output, depending on what the display shows.

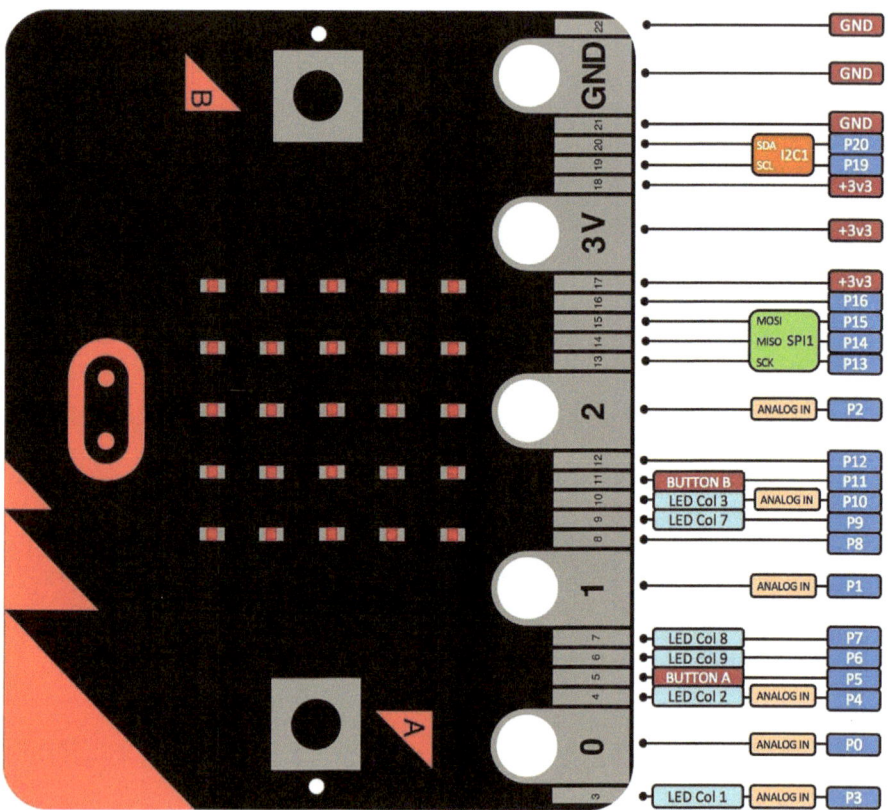

Figure 2-4. *GPIO pins 3, 4, 6, 7, 9, and 10 are connecting to the LED screen*

You can turn on the display again by issuing the **display.on()** function. This will bring the display back to the normal state. You can also get the status of the display with the **display.is_on()** function. It returns true if the display is on and false if the display is off.

Listing 2-5 shows the code that turns off a display for a GPIO mode, waits two seconds, and then turns it on again.

Listing 2-5. Turning the LED Display On and Off

```
from microbit import *
display.scroll("Turning display off")
sleep(100)
display.off() # turn off the display and goes to GPIO mode
sleep(5000)
display.on() # trun on the display
if display.is_on():
    display.scroll("Display back on")
```

Using Built-in Images

The MicroPython Image class offers 63 built-in images that are ready to use with your code. Listing 2-6 presents the full list of built-in images that you can use with the micro:bit.

Listing 2-6. Built-In Images

```
Image.HEART
Image.HEART_SMALL
Image.HAPPY
Image.SMILE
Image.SAD
Image.CONFUSED
Image.ANGRY
Image.ASLEEP
Image.SURPRISED
Image.SILLY
Image.FABULOUS
```

```
Image.MEH
Image.YES
Image.NO
Image.CLOCK12, Image.CLOCK11, Image.CLOCK10, Image.CLOCK9,
Image.CLOCK8, Image.CLOCK7, Image.CLOCK6, Image.CLOCK5, Image.
CLOCK4, Image.CLOCK3, Image.CLOCK2, Image.CLOCK1
Image.ARROW_N, Image.ARROW_NE, Image.ARROW_E, Image.ARROW_SE,
Image.ARROW_S, Image.ARROW_SW, Image.ARROW_W, Image.ARROW_NW
Image.TRIANGLE
Image.TRIANGLE_LEFT
Image.CHESSBOARD
Image.DIAMOND
Image.DIAMOND_SMALL
Image.SQUARE
Image.SQUARE_SMALL
Image.RABBIT
Image.COW
Image.MUSIC_CROTCHET
Image.MUSIC_QUAVER
Image.MUSIC_QUAVERS
Image.PITCHFORK
Image.XMAS
Image.PACMAN
Image.TARGET
Image.TSHIRT
Image.ROLLERSKATE
Image.DUCK
Image.HOUSE
Image.TORTOISE
Image.BUTTERFLY
Image.STICKFIGURE
```

```
Image.GHOST
Image.SWORD
Image.GIRAFFE
Image.SKULL
Image.UMBRELLA
Image.SNAKE
```

With MicroPython, any image can be displayed using the `display.show()` function. The `display.show()` function takes an image as an input and displays it on the LED screen.

Listing 2-7 shows the MicroPython code to display the built-in image named BUTTERFLY on the micro:bit display.

Listing 2-7. Displaying the BUTTERFLY Built-In Image

```
from microbit import *
display.show(Image.BUTTERFLY)
```

Now, flash and run this code on micro:bit, and you should see a butterfly image being displayed on the LED grid, as shown in Figure 2-5.

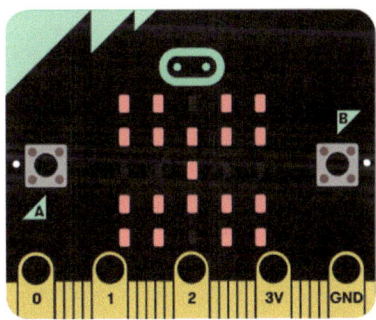

Figure 2-5. *Butterfly image*

As an exercise, you can modify the code to display other built-in images and see how they are displayed on the grid.

In the next section, you learn about creating custom images.

Creating Your Own Images

The Image class of the MicroPython allows you to build your own images. The following steps guide you through how to create an image and convert it to code.

1. Start with a 5x5 grid and fill each square based on how you would like it lit.

2. To encode the image, read each square on each line of the grid using the following rules:

   • If the square is empty, it has the value of 0.

   • If the square is filled, it has the value of the brightness required from 1 to 9.

In this example, learn how to create a custom image to display a **fish** on the micro:bit screen.

1. Draw a 5x5 grid on paper and fill each square so that it forms the shape of a fish (see Figure 2-6).

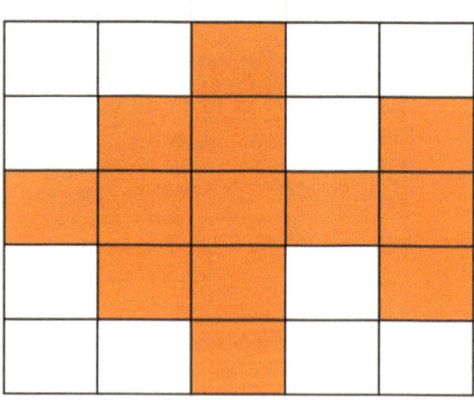

Figure 2-6. *Creating the shape of a fish*

2. Encode each empty square with 0 (off) and each filled square with 9 (the maximum brightness level), as shown in Figure 2-7.

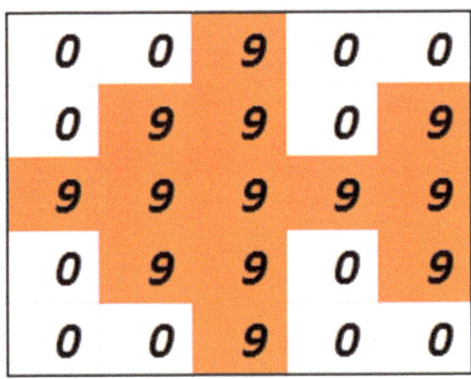

Figure 2-7. *Encoding squares*

3. Write the encoded values of each row as shown here.

    00900
    09909
    99999
    09909
    00900

4. Place each encoded line into code format. Each entry should end with a colon, except for the last line, and be placed within double quotes, as shown here.

    "00900:""09909:""99999:""09909:""00900"

5. Name the image (such as FISH) and assign the
    encoded line:

    ```
    FISH = Image ("00900:""09909:""99999:""09909:""00900")
    ```

6. Display the image using the display.show()
    function:

    ```
    display.show(FISH)
    ```

Listing 2-8 shows the complete code to display the fish image with its
maximum brightness level, which is 9.

Listing 2-8. Custom Image Called FISH

```
from microbit import *

FISH = Image("00900:"
             "09909:"
             "99999:"
             "09909:"
             "00900")

display.show(FISH)
```

You can vary the brightness of each LED to create different shades
on the image. Figure 2-8 shows the same example marked with different
brightness levels.

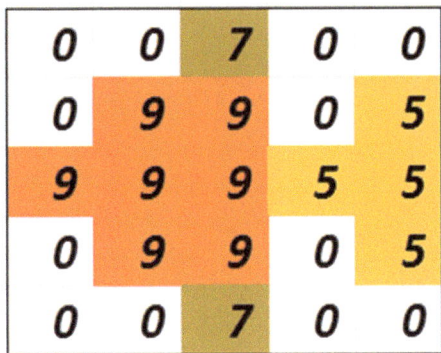

Figure 2-8. *Applying different brightness levels*

The image uses brightness level 9 for the body, 7 for the fins, and 5 for the tail to create different shades. Brightness level 0 is used to create the background by turning off other LEDs. Listing 2-9 shows the modified code.

Listing 2-9. Applying Different Brightness Levels

```
from microbit import *

FISH = Image("00700:"
             "09905:"
             "99955:"
             "09905:"
             "00700")

display.show(FISH)
```

Lists and Animations

The MicroPython image library has two pre-built image lists—ALL_ CLOCKS and ALL_ARROWS. Listings 2-10 and 2-11 present a list of images included with each of the pre-built image lists.

Listing 2-10. ALL_ CLOCKS

```
Image.CLOCK12, Image.CLOCK11, Image.CLOCK10, Image.CLOCK9,
Image.CLOCK8, Image.CLOCK7, Image.CLOCK6, Image.CLOCK5, Image.
CLOCK4, Image.CLOCK3, Image.CLOCK2, Image.CLOCK1
```

Listing 2-11. ALL_ARROWS

```
Image.ARROW_N, Image.ARROW_NE, Image.ARROW_E, Image.ARROW_SE,
Image.ARROW_S, Image.ARROW_SW, Image.ARROW_W, Image.ARROW_NW
```

The display.show() command can display all the images in the list in sequence. Listing 2-12 shows the complete code to display and animate the built-in image list, ALL_CLOCKS.

Listing 2-12. Displaying a Clock Using the Built-In Image List

```
from microbit import *
display.show(Image.ALL_CLOCKS, loop=True, delay=100)
```

The ALL_CLOCKS image list consists of 12 images that can be used to display each hour from 1 to 12. The loop = true runs the animation forever and the delay=100 will slow down the speed of the animation.

If you want, you can display a selected image from the image list, as all image lists are based on a 0 index. As an example, the 12 images in the ALL_CLOCKS list are indexed from 0 to 11, as shown here.

CLOCK12: index 0

CLOCK1: index 1

CLOCK2: index 2

CLOCK3: index 3

CLOCK4: index 4

CLOCK5: index 5

CLOCK6: index 6

CLOCK7: index 7

CLOCK8: index 8

CLOCK9: index 9

CLOCK10: index 10

CLOCK11: index 11

Listing 2-13 shows the code that displays the CLOCK6 image, which is located at index 6 in the ALL_CLOCKS list.

Listing 2-13. Displaying CLOCK6 Image

```
from microbit import *
display.show(Image.ALL_CLOCKS[6]) # index 6 for CLOCK6
```

Listing 2-14 shows the code to animate a clock using image indexes /indices.

Listing 2-14. Animate Images Using Image Indexes

```
from microbit import *
for x in range(0,12):
    display.show(Image.ALL_CLOCKS[x])
    sleep(100)
```

The code in Listing 2-14 will show each CLOCK image, starting from 12 hours to 11 hours (12, 1, 2 , .., 10, 11). You can press the RESET button to start the animation from the beginning or add a while True statement to the code.

You can create custom image lists with the pre-built images. For example, the list named SPOOKY has three pre-built images—GHOST, SWORD, and SKULL.

```
spooky = [Image.GHOST, Image.SWORD, Image.SKULL]
```

You can simply create an animation with this list, as shown in Listing 2-15. The animation will run forever and display each image for one second.

Listing 2-15. Displaying a Spooky Image List

```
from microbit import *
spooky = [Image.GHOST, Image.SWORD, Image.SKULL]

display.show(spooky, loop=True, delay=1000)
```

You can arrange the sequence of images to make an animation by adding a delay between them. Listing 2-16 shows the code that displays a simple animation on micro:bit with two heart images.

Listing 2-16. Display a Beating Heart

```
from microbit import *
while True:
    display.show(Image.HEART)
    sleep(500)
    display.show(Image.HEART_SMALL)
    sleep(500)
```

First, the HEART image will appear on the screen for 500 milliseconds. Then the HEART_SMALL image will appear on the screen for 500 milliseconds. The while True statement will continually repeat these two images on the screen. This will create a blinking effect.

Listing 2-17 shows the code that displays an animated clock with 12 individual CLOCK images.

Listing 2-17. Displaying a Clock with Individual Images

```
from microbit import *
while True:
    display.show(Image.CLOCK12)
    sleep(100)
    display.show(Image.CLOCK1)
    sleep(100)
    display.show(Image.CLOCK2)
    sleep(100)
    display.show(Image.CLOCK3)
    sleep(100)
    display.show(Image.CLOCK4)
    sleep(100)
    display.show(Image.CLOCK5)
    sleep(100)
    display.show(Image.CLOCK6)
    sleep(100)
    display.show(Image.CLOCK7)
    sleep(100)
    display.show(Image.CLOCK8)
    sleep(100)
    display.show(Image.CLOCK9)
    sleep(100)
    display.show(Image.CLOCK10)
    sleep(100)
    display.show(Image.CLOCK11)
    sleep(100)
    display.show(Image.CLOCK12)
```

In this code, the display.show() function is used to display each clock image in the list for 100 milliseconds using the sleep() function. The while True statement creates a continuous loop and animates the hour hand of the clock to move clock-wise.

Custom Animation

If you have a series of custom built images, you can display them in a loop and generate a simple animation based on the custom image, FISH. Let's create a series of images to move the fish from right to left on the LED display. Figure 2-9 shows the image sequence to move the fish to the left from its initial position, which will simulate the swimming effect.

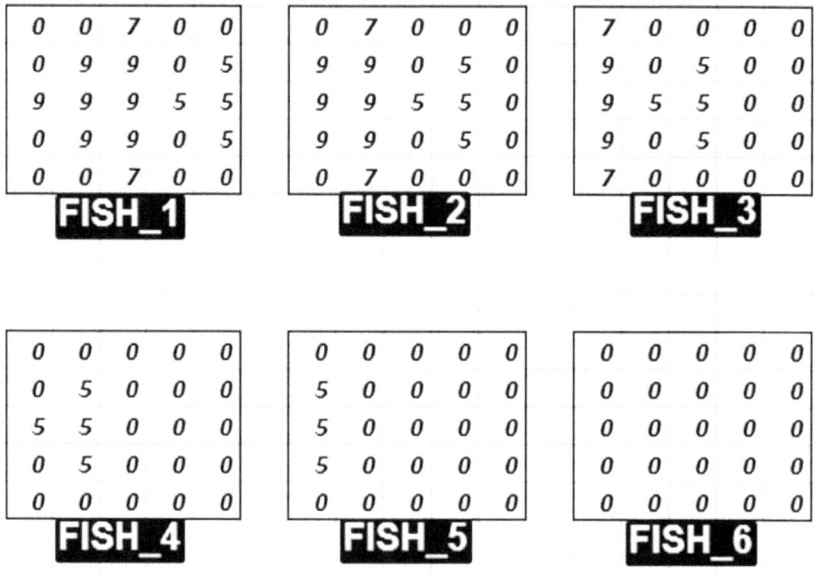

Figure 2-9. *Image frames for animating the FISH*

Listing 2-18 shows the complete code needed to create the animation.

Listing 2-18. Creating a Set of Custom Images and Animating Them

```
from microbit import *

FISH_1 = Image("00700:"
               "09905:"
               "99955:"
               "09905:"
               "00700")

FISH_2 = Image("07000:"
               "99050:"
               "99550:"
               "99050:"
               "07000")

FISH_3 = Image("70000:"
               "90500:"
               "95500:"
               "90500:"
               "70000")

FISH_4 = Image("00000:"
               "05000:"
               "55000:"
               "05000:"
               "00000")

FISH_5 = Image("00000:"
               "50000:"
               "50000:"
               "50000:"
               "00000")
```

```
FISH_6 = Image("00000:"
                "00000:"
                "00000:"
                "00000:"
                "00000")

ALL_FISH = [FISH_1, FISH_2, FISH_3, FISH_4, FISH_5, FISH_6]
display.show(ALL_FISH, loop=True, delay=250)
```

The ALL_FISH list holds six image frames that can be used to emulate the swimming effect. The delay is set to 250 milliseconds to slow down the speed of the animation. The loop=True statement causes the animation to run forever.

Summary

In this chapter, you learned how to work with images and with the LED display. You displayed built-in images and custom images on the micro:bit LED display. Then you created animations based on the pre-built image lists and custom image lists. Finally, you controlled the LED display with a set of core display functions.

The next chapter explains how to work with buttons to get user inputs and control the execution flow of a program.

CHAPTER 3

Working with Buttons

By now, you should be fairly comfortable with micro:bit LED display, images, and animations.

In this chapter, you learn how to use the two built-in buttons on the front of the micro:bit board. You also learn how to connect external buttons to handle user inputs and control the execution flow of a program according to the button events.

Built-in Buttons

The micro:bit board has two built-in momentary pushbuttons soldered on the front of the board, labeled A and B. Button A is internally coupled to digital pin 5 and button B is internally coupled to digital pin 11. You will learn about input/output (I/O) pins in Chapter 4. Figure 3-1 shows the two pushbuttons.

© Pradeeka Seneviratne 2018
P. Seneviratne, *Beginning BBC micro:bit*, https://doi.org/10.1007/978-1-4842-3360-3_3

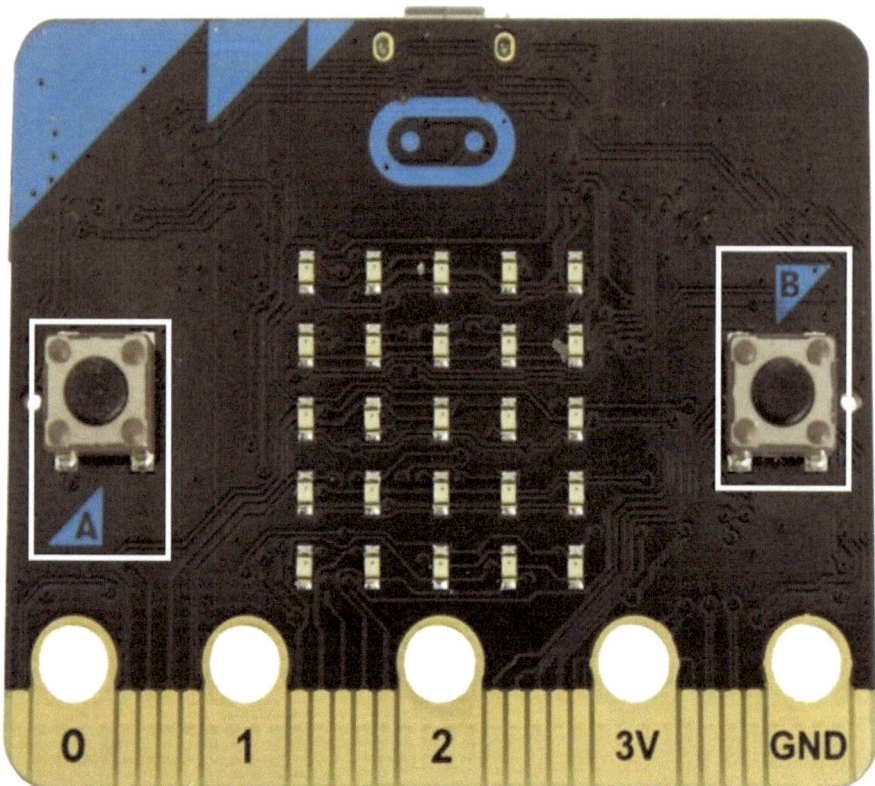

Figure 3-1. *Built-in buttons, A and B*

Handling User Input with Buttons

Buttons can be used to access user input while running the code and make decisions accordingly. The MicroPython library provides some useful methods to interact with the two built-in buttons. Here is the list of these methods:

- `button_a.is_pressed()`
- `button_a.was_pressed()`
- `button_a.get_presses()`

- button_b.is_pressed()

- button_b.was_pressed()

- button_b.get_presses()

Button Is Pressed

First, you'll learn how to check whether a button is being pressed by the user using the is_pressed() method. This method will return true if the button is pressed, and false otherwise. This event is only raised when the button is being pressed and held.

Listing 3-1 shows the code used to detect whether button A is pressed. When you press and hold button A, the LED display will show a HAPPY face; otherwise, the LED display will show a SAD face.

Listing 3-1. Check whether a button is pressed

```
from microbit import *

while True:
    if button_a.is_pressed():
        display.show(Image.HAPPY)
    else:
        display.show(Image.SAD)
```

The while True statement creates an infinite loop that helps you detect the button's situation. The is_pressed() method returns true if the button is pressed and returns false otherwise.

Listing 3-2 shows you how to exit from an infinite loop with the break statement.

Listing 3-2. Check whether a button is pressed and exit from the while True loop

```
from microbit import *

while True:
    if button_a.is_pressed():
        display.show(Image.HAPPY)
    elif button_b.is_pressed():
        break
    else:
        display.show(Image.SAD)

display.clear()
```

With this code, when you press button B, the execution flow of the program will exit from the while True loop and execute the display.clear() method. You can then press the RESET button to start the program from the beginning.

Listing 3-3 presents the code that detects whether buttons A and B are being pressed at the same time. The logical and statement can be used to check whether both conditions are true.

Listing 3-3. Check whether two buttons are being pressed at the same time

```
from microbit import *

while True:
    if button_a.is_pressed() and button_b.is_pressed():
        display.scroll("AB")
    elif button_a.is_pressed():
        display.scroll("A")
    elif button_b.is_pressed():
        display.scroll("B")
    sleep(100)
```

Button Was Pressed

The was_pressed() method returns true after pressing a button. The code shown in Listing 3-4 detects the release event of button A.

Listing 3-4. Check whether a button was pressed

```
from microbit import *

while True:
    if button_a.was_pressed():
        display.show(Image.HAPPY)
    else:
        display.show(Image.SAD)
    sleep(3000)
```

When you run this code on the micro:bit, initially the LED display will show a SAD face. If you press button A, the HAPPY image will display on the LED screen for three seconds, a duration defined by the sleep method. Otherwise, it will display a SAD image until you press button A again. If you press button A while the program is sleeping, it will not immediately be detected by the program, but it will be detected in the next iteration of the program.

Button Presses

The get_presses() method returns the number of times a button has been pressed. The code shown in Listing 3-5 can be used to count the number of times button A has been pressed.

Listing 3-5. Counts the number of times a button has been pressed

```
from microbit import *

while True:
    sleep(10000)
    display.scroll(str(button_a.get_presses()))
```

The sleep function is used to pause the program. During that time, the program counts the number of times the user pressed button A. You can increase the delay time to get more button presses. Finally, the get_presses() method returns the number of times button A has been pressed. The str() function converts the numeric value from button_a. get_presses() to a string to scroll on the display.

Connecting External Buttons

micro:bit has two built-in pushbuttons called *momentary* pushbuttons. You can use external buttons to replace them or increase the number of buttons to handle more user inputs.

Momentary Pushbuttons

Typically, a momentary pushbutton has four pins, as shown in the Figure 3-2.

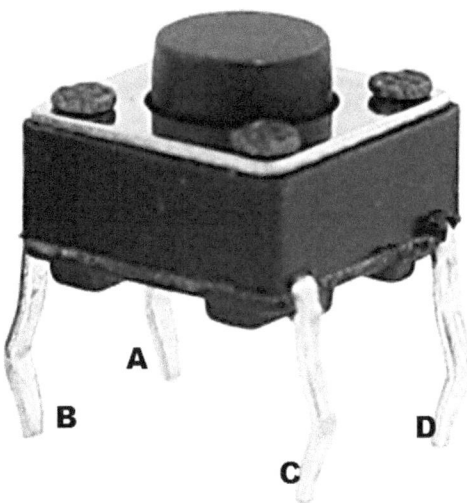

Figure 3-2. *Pinout of the momentary pushbutton*

The internal connection between the four pins is shown in the Figure 3-3.

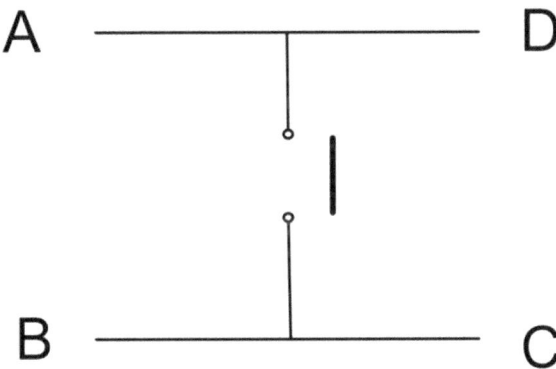

Figure 3-3. *Internal connection between pins*

These switches are normally in the OPEN state and you must be pushed to complete or close the circuit. The circuit can be completed through AB, CD, AC, or BD.

Using External Buttons

You can replace the two built-in buttons with external momentary pushbuttons. Button A is internally connected to pin 5 and button B is internally connected to the pin 11. Pins 5 and 11 have pull-up resistors, which means that by default they use a voltage of 3V.

Figure 3-4 shows how to connect external momentary pushbuttons to the micro:bit to use the functions of built-in buttons A and B. You do not need to use extra pull-up resistors because pins 5 and 11 have built-in pull-up resistors. You can easily access the micro:bit's pins 5 and 11 by plugging the micro:bit in to an edge connector breakout (see Chapter 4 for more information).

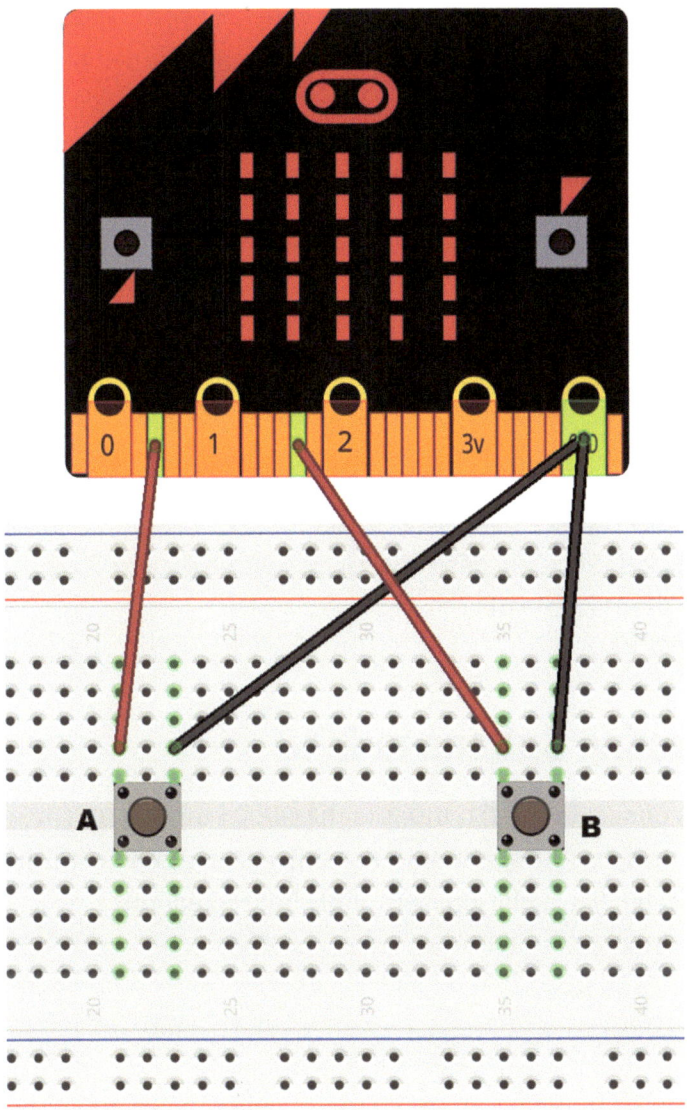

Figure 3-4. *Connecting external buttons for built-in buttons A and B*

Listing 3-6 shows the MicroPython code that you can use to test the behavior of the new external buttons. The same code can be found in Listing 3-3.

Listing 3-6. Using external buttons

```
from microbit import *

while True:
    if button_a.is_pressed() and button_b.is_pressed():
        display.scroll("AB")
        break
    elif button_a.is_pressed():
        display.scroll("A")
    elif button_b.is_pressed():
        display.scroll("B")
    sleep(100)
```

Connecting Buttons to GPIO

You can connect external buttons to the GPIO pins 0 to 16. The wiring diagram in Figure 3-5 shows how to connect a momentary pushbutton with GPIO pin 0 to a pull-up resistor of about 1 kiloohm.

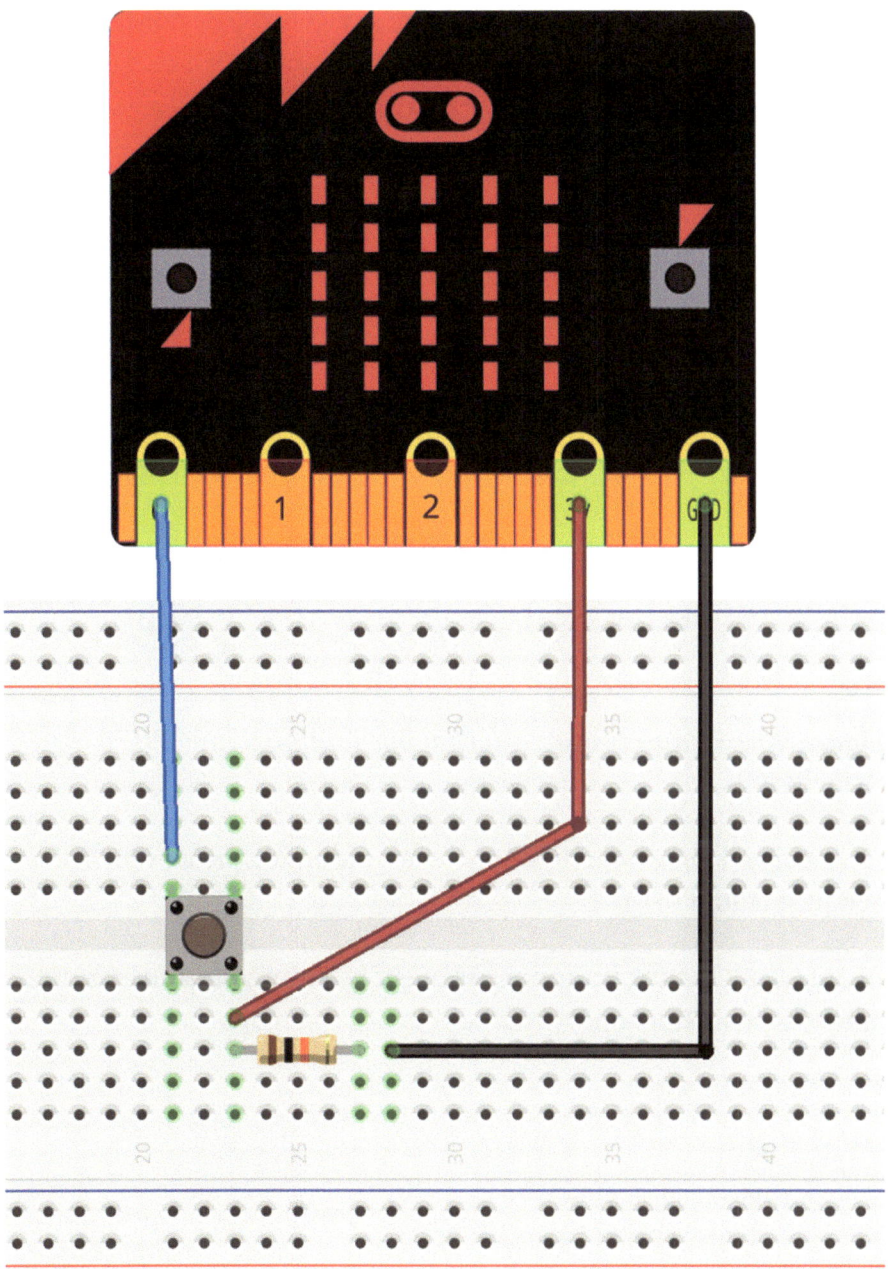

Figure 3-5. *Connecting an external pushbutton with GPIO 0 (wiring diagram)*

The schematic for the wiring diagram in Figure 3-5 is shown in Figure 3-6.

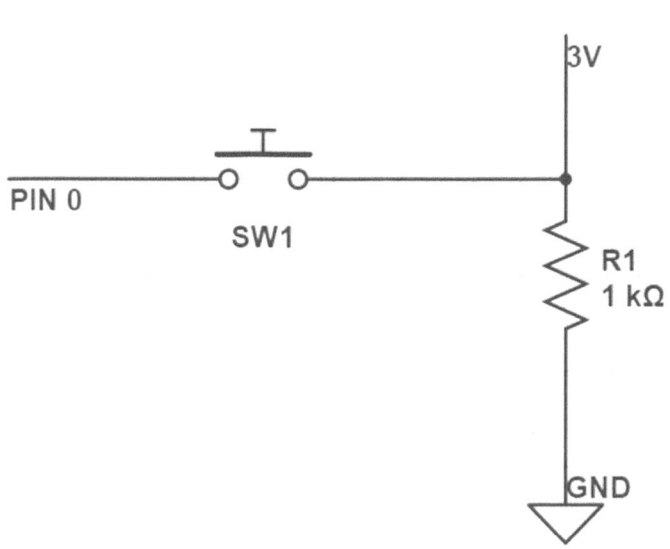

Figure 3-6. *Connecting an external pushbutton with GPIO 0 (schematic)*

Listing 3-7 shows the code used to test the button press event of the new pushbutton.

Listing 3-7. Testing button press event by connecting an external button with a GPIO pin

```
from microbit import *

while True:
    if pin0.read_digital():
        display.show(Image.HAPPY)
    else:
        display.show(Image.SAD)
```

The read_digital() method returns 1 (true for 3V) or 0 (false for 0V), depending on the voltage level of pin 0. When you press and hold the pushbutton, the voltage level of pin 0 becomes 3V and the HAPPY image appears on the LED screen. When you release the pushbutton, the voltage level of pin 0 becomes 0V and the SAD image appears.

You can use crocodile clips to connect external components to the large pads (GPIOs 0, 1, and 2) of the micro:bit edge connector. If you want to connect wires to small pads of the edge connector to access other GPIO pins, the easiest way is to use an edge connector breakout. You will learn how to use an edge connector breakout with micro:bit in Chapter 4, "Using Inputs and Outputs".

Summary

In this chapter, you learned about the micro:bit built-in buttons, button events, and the use of external buttons.

The next chapter explains how to use inputs and outputs with a micro:bit edge connector and connect devices with communication protocols such as SPI, UART, and I2C.

CHAPTER 4

Using Inputs and Outputs

In this chapter, you learn how to handle inputs and outputs with micro:bit through the edge connector. The 21 I/O pins can be used to work with analog, digital, I2C, SPI, and UART. Some I/O pins are also specialized to build touch-sensitive applications. The micro:bit only exposes three I/O pins through the edge connector for basic users. If you want to access the full set of I/O pins, you can use the edge connector breakout board.

Edge Connector

micro:bit exposes its I/O pins through the edge connector, as shown in Figure 4-1. The edge connector consists of large and small connection pads. The large connection pads expose GPIO pins 0, 1, and 2 only.

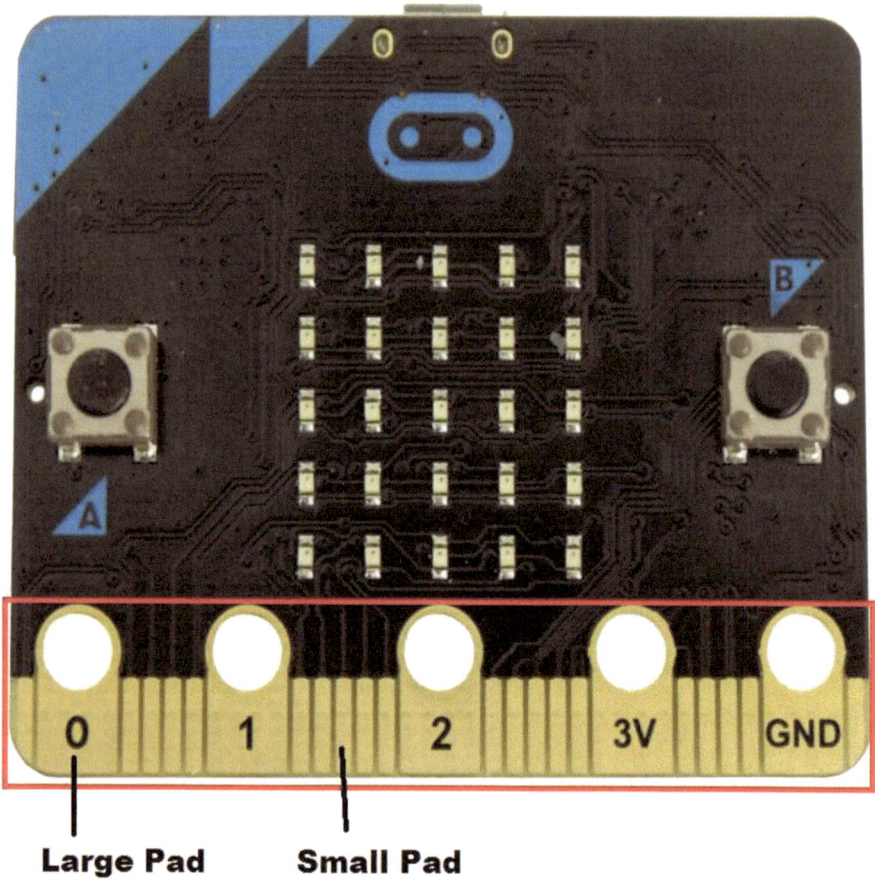

Figure 4-1. *Edge connector with large and small pads (image source: micro:bit Foundation)*

Using an Edge Connector Breakout Board

For practical use, the small pads in the edge connector are difficult to access with crocodile clips. As a solution, you can use an edge connector breakout board to access all 21 I/O pins. The micro:bit pins are broken into a row of pin headers. You can use male-to-female jumper wires to connect the pin headers. The I2C pin (pins 19 and 20) are separated from the pin header and exposed as solderable pads. Figure 4-2 shows the edge connector breakout board.

Figure 4-2. *Edge connector breakout board (image courtesy of Kitronik: https://www.kitronik.co.uk/)*

There are four major areas in the edge connector breakout board, as shown in Figure 4-3.

- *BBC micro:bit compatible connector*: This is the slot where you insert the edge connector side of the micro:bit board.

- *I2C pins*: Solder pads connected to the micro:bit I2C pins 19 and 20.

- *Pin headers*: The 20x2 row of pin headers connected through the micro:bit pin numbers, as indicated. You can connect IDC cable or jumper wires to make connections.

- *Prototyping area*: Allows you to prototype simple circuits in this area with switches, sensors, and any pull-up or pull-down resistors. The area consists of 3V and 0V rows, and three additional connecting sections.

Figure 4-3. *Major areas of the edge connector breakout board (image courtesy of Kitronik:* `https://www.kitronik.co.uk/`)

Figure 4-4 shows how to insert the micro:bit board into the edge connector breakout board. Make sure to insert it firmly into the slot; the side of the LED matrix should be face up.

Figure 4-4. *Inserting micro:bit into the edge connector breakout board (image courtesy of Kitronik:* `https://www.kitronik.co.uk/`*)*

Experimenting with I/O Pins

The 21 I/O pins can be categorized in to three types: touch, analog, and digital. Furthermore, some digital pins are specialized to use with serial communication protocols such as I2C, SPI, and UART. Figure 4-5 shows the type of pins and usage.

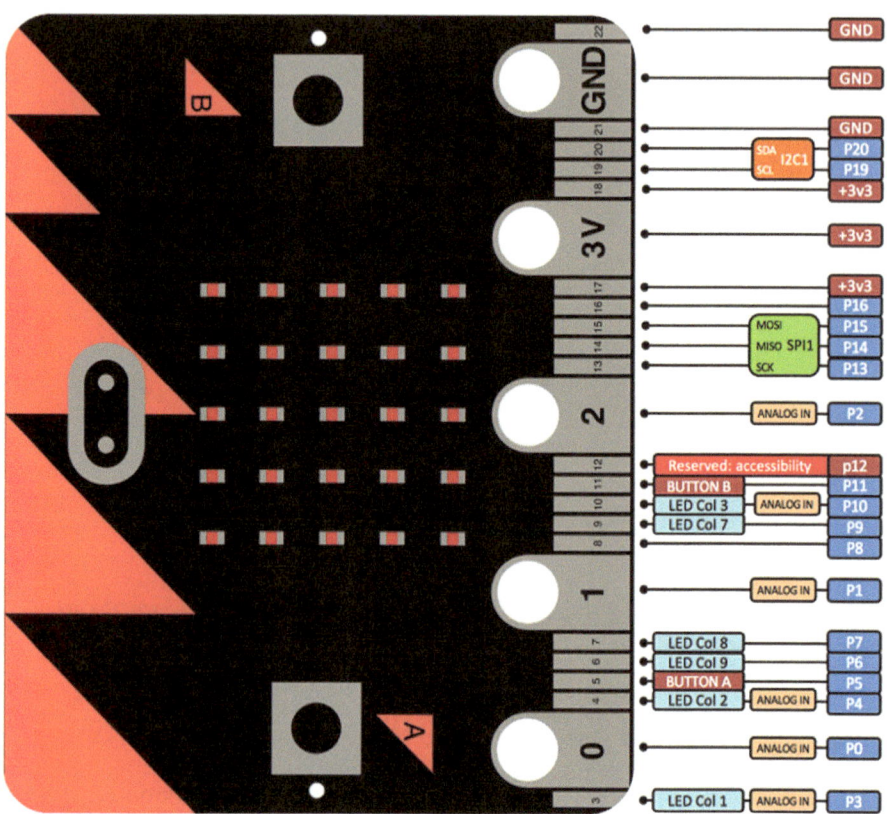

Figure 4-5. *Type of pins and usage (image courtesy of micro:bit Foundation:* http://microbit.org/*)*

Table 4-1 shows the type and function of each pin.

Table 4-1. *Type and Function of micro:bit I/O Pins*

Pin	Name	Description
22	0V	0V/GND
0V	0V	0V/GND
21	0V	0V/GND
20	SDA	Serial data pin connected to the magnetometer and accelerometer connected through I2C bus
19	SCL	Serial clock pin connected to the magnetometer and accelerometer through I2C bus
18	3V	3V/positive supply
3V	3V	3V/positive supply
17	3V	3V/positive supply
16	DIO	General purpose digital I/O
15	MOSI	Serial connection: master output/slave input
14	MISO	Serial connection: master input/slave output
13	SCK	Serial connection clock
2	PAD2	General purpose digital/analog I/O
12	DIO	General purpose digital I/O
11	BTN_B	Button B: normally high, goes low on pressing
10	COL3	Column 3 on the LED matrix
9	COL7	Column 7 on the LED matrix
8	DIO	General purpose digital I/O
1	PAD1	General purpose digital/analog I/O
7	COL8	Column 8 on the LED matrix

(continued)

Table 4-1. (*continued*)

Pin	Name	Description
6	COL9	Column 9 on the LED matrix
5	BTN_A	Button A: normally high, goes low on pressing
4	COL2	Column 2 on the LED matrix
0	PAD0	General purpose digital/analog I/O
3	COL1	Column 1 on the LED matrix

Source: Kitronik at `https://www.kitronik.co.uk/`

Touch

Micro:bit board has three specialized pins with large connector pads, known as touch pins. Figure 4-6 shows the touch pins that you can use to build touch-sensitive applications based on the analog input. They are pins 0, 1, and 2. The large connector pads allow you to touch them with your fingertips to change the capacitance. To apply the electrical capacitance of your body on a touch pin, first touch and hold the GND pin followed by the touch pin associated with your application.

Figure 4-6. *Touch pins*

Figure 4-7 shows how to touch and hold the GND pin and pin 0.

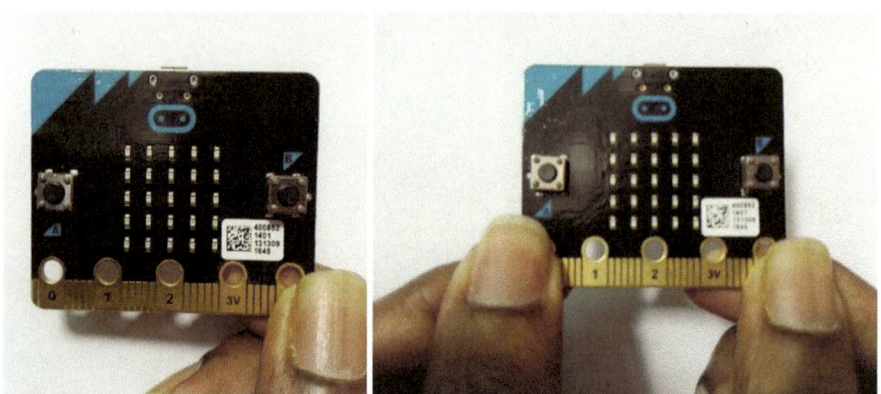

Figure 4-7. *First hold the GND pad (left); then touch the pin 0 pad (right)*

Listing 4-1 presents simple MicroPython code that can be used to sense the electrical capacitance of the human body by touching pin 0. If you touch the ground pin with pin 0, the LED screen will show a HAPPY image; otherwise, it will show a SAD image.

Listing 4-1. Detecting human touch

```
from microbit import *

while True:
    if pin0.is_touched():
        display.show(Image.HAPPY)
    else:
        display.show(Image.SAD)
```

The micro:bit TouchPin class provides the is_touched() method, which returns True if the pin is being touched with a finger, and returns False otherwise. The show() method of the display class is used to display images on the LED screen.

When you touch a touch pad, the capacitance on the pad will increase. You can determine the capacitance on a touch pad using the read_analog() method. It will return a value between 0-1023.

Listing 4-2 shows the MicroPython code that reads the capacitance on pin 0.

Listing 4-2. Reading capacitance on pin 0

```
from microbit import *
while True:
        display.scroll(str(pin0.read_analog()))
        sleep(100)
```

Analog Input and Output

You can use the same large touch pads to build circuits with analog input and output. First, prepare with following components to build the circuit.

- A 10kiloohm potentiometer

- Three wires with crocodile clips attached to both sides

- A 3mm LED

Figure 4-8 shows the wiring diagram for the circuit.

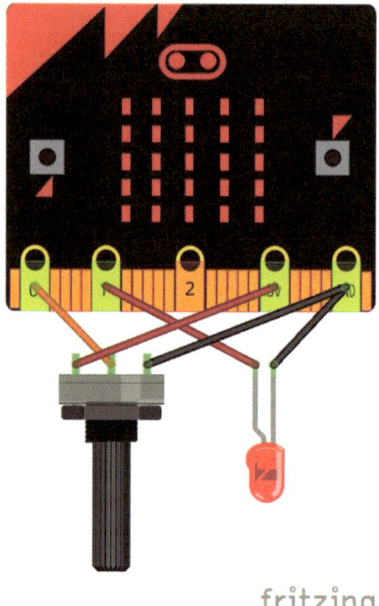

Figure 4-8. *Wiring diagram for the analog read/write circuit*

Follow these steps to wire the circuit.

1. Connect the positive lead of the LED to micro:bit pin 1.

2. Connect the negative lead of the LED to the micro:bit GND pin.

3. Connect the middle pin of the potentiometer to micro:bit pin 0.

4. Connect one of the outer pins of the potentiometer to micro:bit 3V.

5. Connect another outer pin of the potentiometer to the micro:bit GND pin.

Listing 4-3 show code that controls the brightness of a LED using a potentiometer.

Listing 4-3. Controlling brightness of a LED

```
from microbit import *

while True:
    pin1.write_analog(pin0.read_analog())
    sleep(100)
```

When you turn the shaft of the potentiometer, the voltage at the center pin will change. The same effect will happen at the micro:bit pin 0. You can read the voltage at the center pin with read_analog() method and write the same value at pin 1 to change the brightness of the LED.

The read_analog() returns an integer between 0-1023. The same value can be passed to the write_analog() method to control the voltage at pin 1, which controls the brightness of the attached LED.

The following steps show you how to calculate voltage on pin 1 for an analog value 500 on pin 0.

First, calculate the voltage for the analog read value 1 by dividing the maximum voltage, 3V, by 1023:

```
3.0 / 1023 = 0.002932551v
```

Then multiply this result by 500:

```
0.002932551 x   500 = 1.46
```

So a value of 500 will send 1.46 volts in to pin 1.

Digital Input and Output

Digital signal or data can be expressed as a series of 0 and 1 digits. Figure 4-9 shows a digital signal with two states over time. The voltage level of HIGH takes 3.3V and LOW takes 0V.

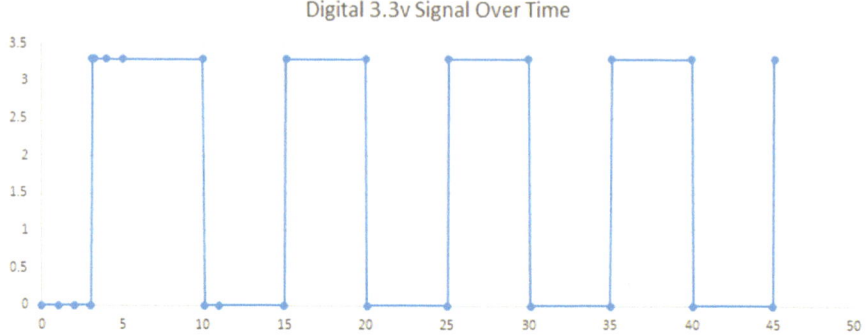

Figure 4-9. *Digital 3.3V signal over time*

You can also use the large touch pads in the edge connector to work with digital signals. By now, you have learned that the large connection pads (pins 0, 1, and 2) support with touch, analog, and digital processing.

First, you learn how to read a button state using digital read and show the button status using an LED. Figure 4-10 shows the wiring diagram.

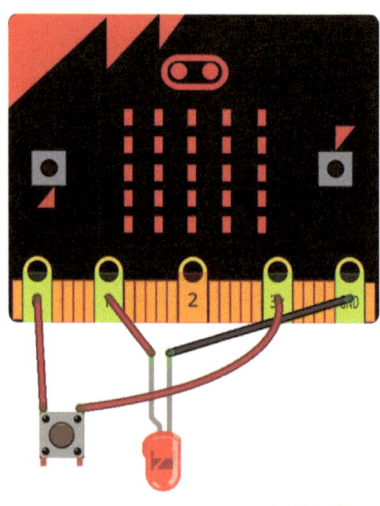

Figure 4-10. *Wiring diagram for a digital read/write circuit*

Follow these steps to make the connections between components.

1. Connect the pushbutton to micro:bit between pin 0 and GND.

2. Connect the positive pin of the LED to micro:bit pin 1.

3. Connect the negative pin of the LED to micro:bit GND.

Listing 4-4 presents the MicroPython code that detects the button state and controls the LED.

Listing 4-4. Detecting button state

```
from microbit import *

while True:
    if pin0.read_digital():
        pin1.write_digital(1)
    else:
        pin1.write_digital(0)
```

When you press and hold the pushbutton, the read_digital() method returns 1. The if statement is used to compare the return value at pin 0.

Alternatively, you can write the if pin0.read_digital():statement as if pin0.read_digital()== 1:. The write_digital() method will change the voltage at pin 1 by writing the value 1 or 0, depending on the button status. In the previous example, the LED will turn on if the button is pressed, and will turn off otherwise.

I2C (Inter-Integrated Circuit)

The micro:bit supports the I2C (inter-integrated circuit) communication protocol that allows you to connect devices through the I2C bus. You can use the SDA and SCL pins of the micro:bit to connect devices and communicate through the I2C bus. Therefore, I2C requires two wires to communicate.

Depending on its configuration, the I2C bus can support up to 1024 slave devices; however, as 7-bit addressing is used with micro:bit MicroPython, the number of slave devices is 128. Figure 4-11 shows the communication paths between the master and slave devices of an I2C bus.

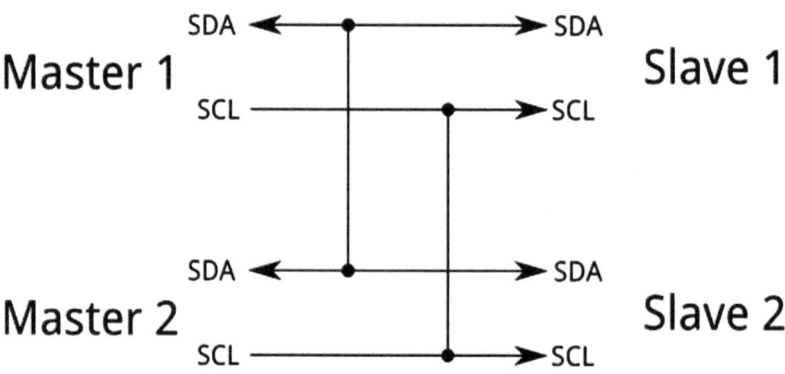

Figure 4-11. *Master and slave devices connected through the I2C bus*

Fortunately, you can learn how to read sensor data through an I2C bus without connecting any I2C capable sensors with the micro:bit. The on-board magnetometer and accelerometer of the micro:bit are internally connected to the I2C bus.

What follows is a quick example of reading data from the accelerometer connected to the I2C bus. The micro:bit uses NXP/Freescale MMA8652FC three-axis 12-bit digital accelerometer sensor. The datasheet for MMA8652FC can be found at `http://www.nxp.com/docs/en/data-sheet/MMA8652FC.pdf`.

Figure 4-12 shows a section of the register address map from the MMA8652FC datasheet.

Name	Type	Register Address	Auto-Increment Address				Default	Hex Value	Comment
			FMODE = 0 F_READ = 0	FMODE > 0 F_READ = 0	FMODE = 0 F_READ = 1	FMODE > 0 F_READ = 1			
STATUS/ F_STATUS[(1)(2)]	R	0x00	0x01				00000000	0x00	FMODE = 0, real time status FMODE > 0, FIFO status
OUT_X_MSB[(1)(2)]	R	0x01	0x02	0x01	0x03	0x01	Output	—	[7:0] are 8 MSBs of 12-bit sample. Root pointer to XYZ FIFO data.
OUT_X_LSB[(1)(2)]	R	0x02	0x03		0x00		Output	—	[7:4] are 4 LSBs of 12-bit real-time sample
OUT_Y_MSB[(1)(2)]	R	0x03	0x04		0x05	0x00	Output	—	[7:0] are 8 MSBs of 12-bit real-time sample
OUT_Y_LSB[(1)(2)]	R	0x04	0x05		0x00		Output	—	[7:4] are 4 LSBs of 12-bit real-time sample
OUT_Z_MSB[(1)(2)]	R	0x05	0x06		0x00		Output	—	[7:0] are 8 MSBs of 12-bit real-time sample
OUT_Z_LSB[(1)(2)]	R	0x06	0x00				Output	—	[7:4] are 4 LSBs of 12-bit real-time sample
Reserved	R	0x07 0x08	—	—	—	—	—	—	Reserved. Read return 0x00.
F_SETUP[(1)(3)]	R/W	0x09	0x0A				00000000	0x00	FIFO setup
TRIG_CFG[(1)(4)]	R/W	0x0A	0x0B				00000000	0x00	Map of FIFO data capture events
SYSMOD[(1)(2)]	R	0x0B	0x0C				00000000	0x00	Current System mode
INT_SOURCE[(1)(2)]	R	0x0C	0x0D				00000000	0x00	Interrupt status
WHO_AM_I[(1)]	R	0x0D	0x0E				01001010	0x4A	Device ID (0x4A)
XYZ_DATA_CFG[(1)(4)]	R/W	0x0E	0x0F				00000000	0x00	Dynamic Range Settings
HP_FILTER_CUTOFF[(1)(4)]	R/W	0x0F	0x10				00000000	0x00	High-Pass Filter Selection

Figure 4-12. *Register address map of the MMA8652FC (source:* `http://www.nxp.com/docs/en/data-sheet/MMA8652FC.pdf`*)*

The measured acceleration data is stored in the following registers as 2's complement 12-bit:

- OUT_X_MSB, OUT_X_LSB

- OUT_Y_MSB, OUT_Y_LSB

- OUT_Z_MSB, OUT_Z_LSB

You can read the measured acceleration data as an 8-bit or 12-bit result. The datasheet says: The most significant eight bits of each axis are stored in OUT_X (Y, Z)_MSB, so applications needing only 8-bit results can use these three registers (and ignore the OUT_X/Y/Z_LSB registers). To use only 8-bit results, the F_READ bit in CTRL_REG1 must be set. When the F_READ bit is cleared, the fast read mode is disabled (see Figure 4-13).

PULSE_TMLT[(1)(4)]	R/W	0x26	0x27	00000000	0x00	Time limit for pulse
PULSE_LTCY[(1)(4)]	R/W	0x27	0x28	00000000	0x00	Latency time for 2nd pulse
PULSE_WIND[(1)(4)]	R/W	0x28	0x29	00000000	0x00	Window time for 2nd pulse
ASLP_COUNT[(1)(4)]	R/W	0x29	0x2A	00000000	0x00	Counter setting for Auto-SLEEP
CTRL_REG1[(1)(4)]	R/W	0x2A	0x2B	00000000	0x00	Data rates and modes setting
CTRL_REG2[(1)(4)]	R/W	0x2B	0x2C	00000000	0x00	Sleep Enable, OS modes, RST, ST
CTRL_REG3[(1)(4)]	R/W	0x2C	0x2D	00000000	0x00	Wake from Sleep, IPOL, PP_OD
CTRL_REG4[(1)(4)]	R/W	0x2D	0x2E	00000000	0x00	Interrupt enable register
CTRL_REG5[(1)(4)]	R/W	0x2E	0x2F	00000000	0x00	Interrupt pin (INT1/INT2) map
OFF_X[(1)(4)]	R/W	0x2F	0x30	00000000	0x00	X-axis offset adjust
OFF_Y[(1)(4)]	R/W	0x30	0x31	00000000	0x00	Y-axis offset adjust
OFF_Z[(1)(4)]	R/W	0x31	0x0D	00000000	0x00	Z-axis offset adjust

Figure 4-13. *CTRL_REG1 register*

According to the datasheet, the I2C device address of the accelerometer is 0x1d (see Figure 4-14).

Pin #	Pin Name	Description	Notes
1	VDD	Power supply	Device power is supplied through the VDD line. Power supply decoupling capacitors should be placed as close as possible to pin 1 and pin 8 of the device.
2	SCL[(1)]	I²C Serial Clock	7-bit I²C device address is 0x1D.
3	INT1	Interrupt 1 output	The interrupt source and pin settings are user-programmable through the I²C interface.
4	BYP	Internal regulator output capacitor connection	
5	INT2	Interrupt 2 output	See INT1.
6	GND	Ground	
7	GND	Ground	
8	VDDIO	Digital Interface Power supply	
9	GND	Ground	
10	SDA[(1)]	I²C Serial Data	See SCL.

Figure 4-14. *I2C device address of the accelerometer chip*

Listing 4-5 shows the MicroPython code that reads the accelerometer data from the x-axis and displays it with REPL in the Mu editor.

Listing 4-5. Reading Accelerometer Data from the X-Axis Through I2C

```
from microbit import *

i2c.write(0x1d, bytes([0x2a,1]), repeat=False)
while True:

    Byte = i2c.read(0x1d, 2) [1]
    print(Byte)

    sleep(100)
```

The code uses the i2c.write() and i2c.read() functions:

```
i2c.read(addr, n, repeat=False)
```

- addr: 7-bit I2C address of your device. In this case, the I2C address of the accelerometer is 0x1d.

- n: Read n bytes.

- repeat: If True, no stop bit will be sent.

  i2c.write(addr, buf, repeat=False)

- addr: 7-bit I2C address of your device. In this case, the I2C address of the accelerometer is 0x1d.

- buf: Write bytes from buffer.

- repeat: If True, no stop bit will be sent.

To use only 8-bit results, the F_READ bit in CTRL_REG1 must be set. You can use the i2c.write() function to write one byte to the register CTRL_REG1 at address 0x2a. The repeat is set to False to send the stop bit. If repeat is True, no stop bit will be sent.

i2c.write(0x1d, bytes([0x2a,1]), repeat=False)

Then, you can read the register, OUT_X_MSB, at address 0x1d. The i2c.read() function can be used to read the first two bytes of the device. However, you only need the byte at index 1, which holds the bytes for the OUT_X_MSB register (see Figure 4-15).

Byte = i2c.read(0x1d, 2) [1]

Name	Type	Register Address	Auto-Increment Address			
			FMODE = 0 F_READ = 0	FMODE > 0 F_READ = 0	FMODE = 0 F_READ = 1	F F
STATUS/ F_STATUS[1][2]	R	0x00	0x01			
OUT_X_MSB[1][2]	R	0x01	0x02	0x01	0x03	
OUT_X_LSB[1][2]	R	0x02	0x03			0x0C
OUT_Y_MSB[1][2]	R	0x03	0x04		0x05	

Figure 4-15. *OUT_X_MSB register at address 0x01*

Finally, print the bytes with the print() function.

```
print(Byte)
```

Figure 4-16 shows the output for this code. After flashing the code to the micro:bit, click on the REPL button in the Mu editor to open and view the REPL window. In some situations, the REPL window only shows a few values and then stops. If you encounter a similar thing, press the RESET button on the micro:bit to restart the program. Pan and tilt the micro:bit board by hand to see the change of the accelerometer values on the x-axis. You learn how to work with and read values from the built-in accelerometer in Chapter 5.

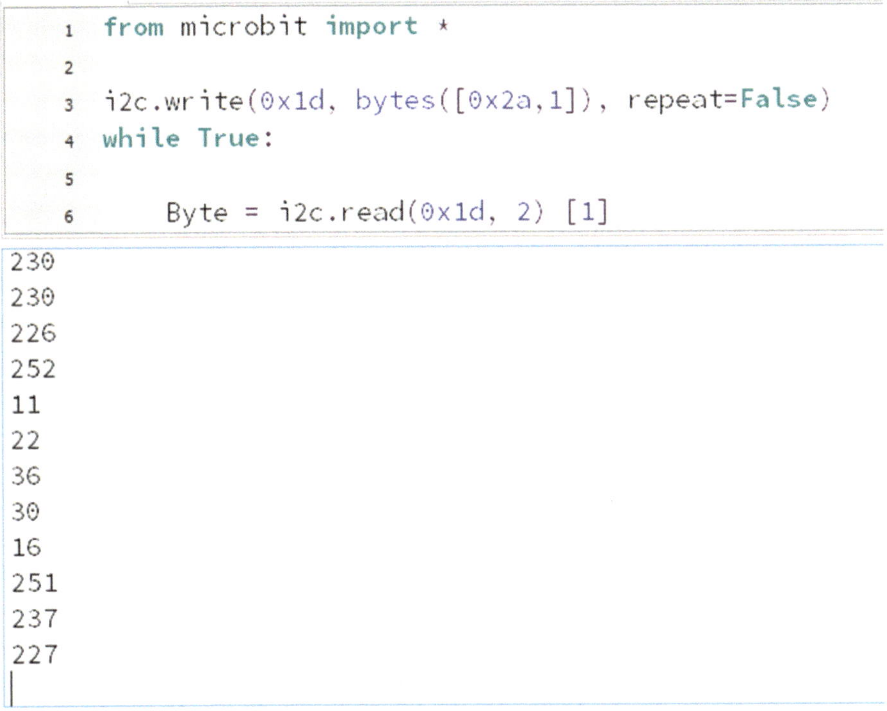

```
1   from microbit import *
2
3   i2c.write(0x1d, bytes([0x2a,1]), repeat=False)
4   while True:
5
6       Byte = i2c.read(0x1d, 2) [1]
230
230
226
252
11
22
36
30
16
251
237
227
```

Figure 4-16. *Reading accelerometer values (values on the x-axis) through I2C*

SPI (Serial Peripheral Interface)

The SPI (serial peripheral interface) allows you to connect devices to the micro:bit through the SPI bus. The SPI uses a master-slave architecture with a single master device. The SPI requires three wires to communicate between the master and slave. They are:

- SCLK: Serial clock (output from master)

- MOSI: Master output, slave input (output from master)

- MISO: Master input, slave output (output from slave)

Now you are going to build a simple circuit with the Adafruit Thermocouple Amplifier MAX31855 breakout board (see Figure 4-17) and micro:bit. Then you will write a simple MicroPython program to read the temperature through the SPI bus.

Figure 4-17. *Adafruit thermocouple amplifier MAX31855 breakout board (image courtesy of Adafruit Industries)*

Additionally, you need a Thermocouple Type-K glass braid insulated-K (see Figure 4-18) or a Thermocouple type-k glass braid insulated stainless steel tip (see Figure 4-19) to connect to the MAX31855 breakout board.

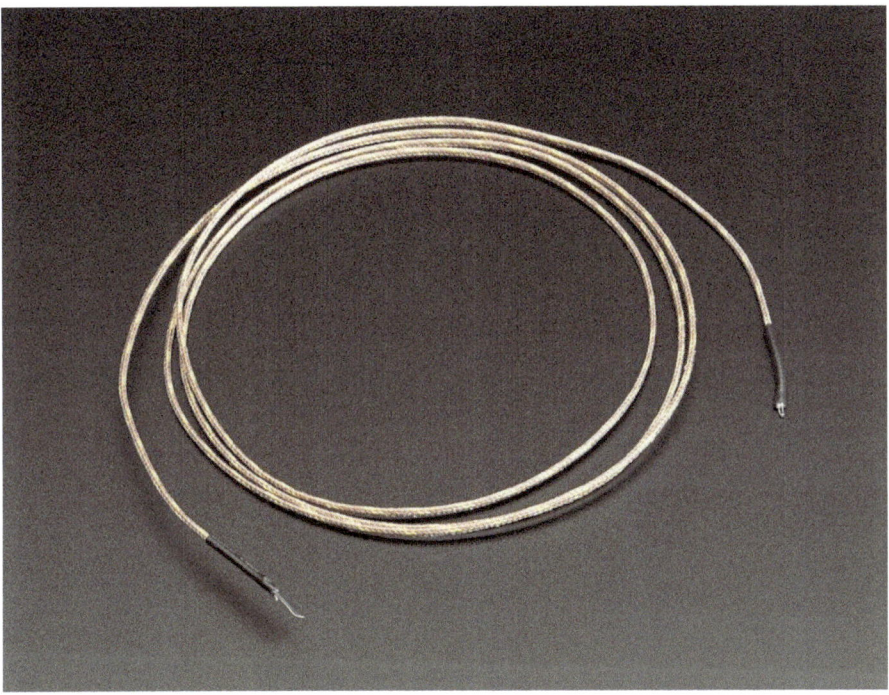

Figure 4-18. *Thermocouple Type-K glass braid insulated-K (https://www.adafruit.com/product/270) (image courtesy of Adafruit Industries)*

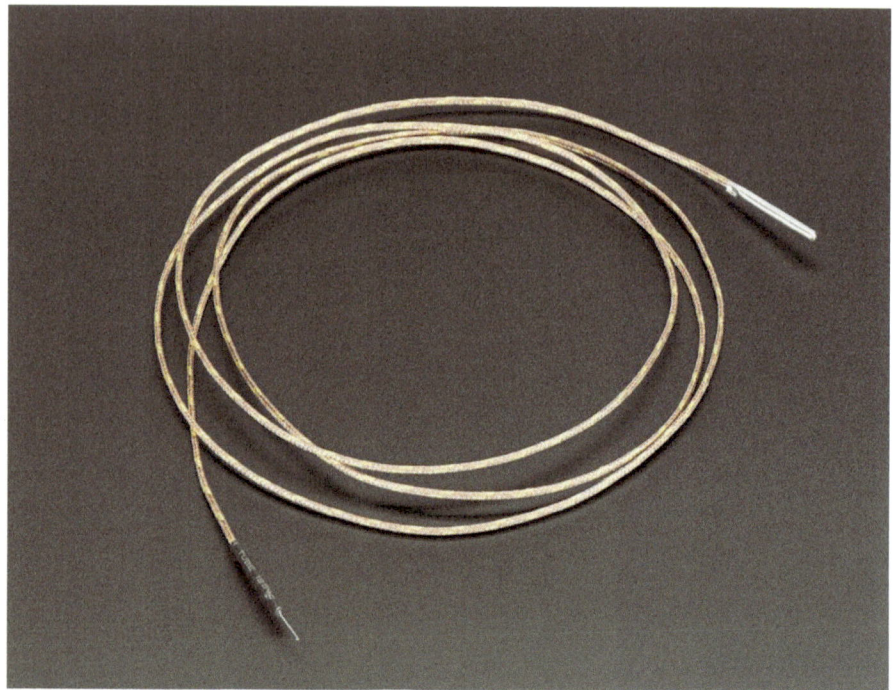

Figure 4-19. *Thermocouple Type-K Glass braid insulated stainless steel tip (*`https://www.adafruit.com/product/3245`*) (Image courtesy of Adafruit Industries)*

Assemble the MAX31855 breakout board with the provided 7-pin header and terminal connector block. Then connect the Thermocouple Type-K glass braid insulated-K or Thermocouple Type-K glass braid insulated stainless steel tip to the terminal connector block. Connect the red wire of the Thermocouple to the connector marked `RED` – and the yellow wire of the Thermocouple to the connector marked `YELLOW` + (see Figure 4-20).

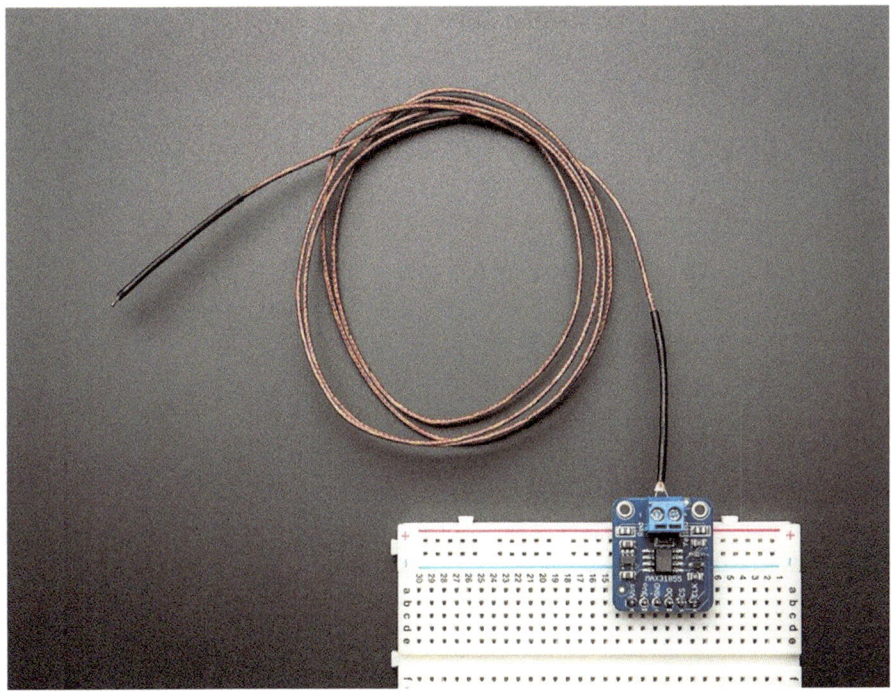

Figure 4-20. *Assembled MAX31855 breakout board with Thermocouple (image courtesy of Adafruit Industries)*

Figure 4-21 shows the wiring diagram that you can use to connect the Adafruit Thermocouple amplifier MAX31855 breakout board and micro:bit together. You can use a micro:bit edge connector breakout board to easily access the SPI pins (SCK and MISO) on the micro:bit. For an enlarged view, see Figure 4-22.

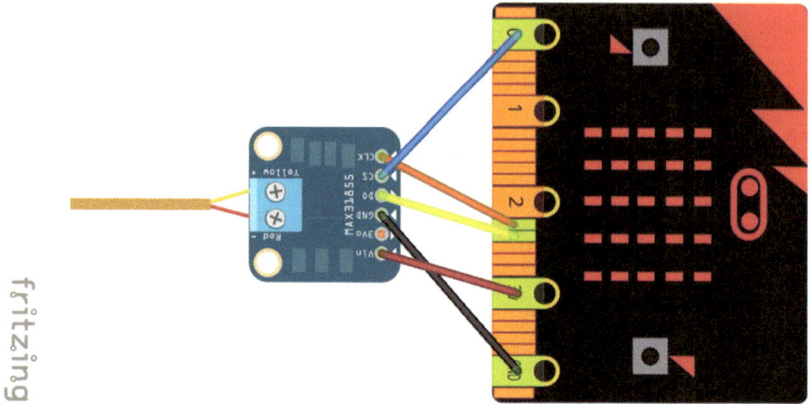

Figure 4-21. *Wiring diagram between the MAX31855 breakout board and micro:bit*

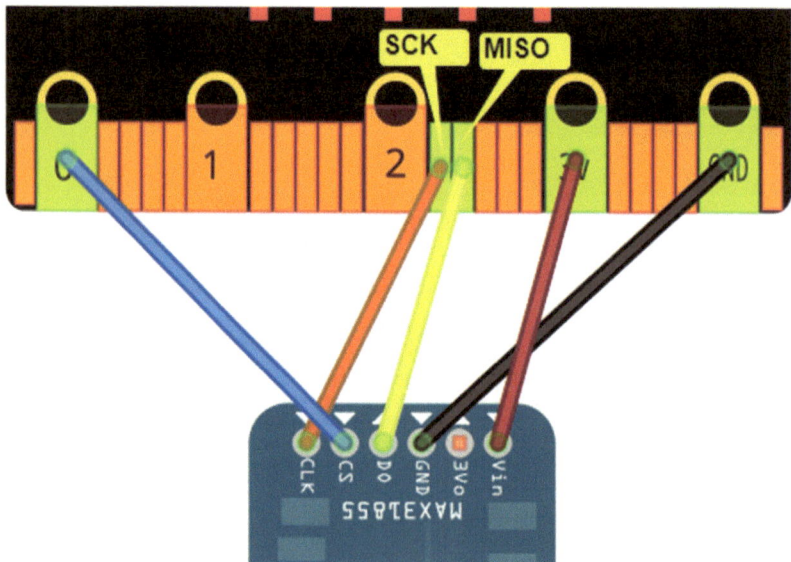

Figure 4-22. *Wiring diagram between the MAX31855 breakout board and micro:bit (enlarged view)*

Follow these steps to easily make connections between the MAX31855 breakout board and micro:bit with wires.

1. Connect the MAX31855 breakout board Vin to micro:bit 3V.

2. Connect the MAX31855 breakout board GND to the micro:bit GND.

3. Connect the MAX31855 breakout board CLK to the micro:bit SCK (pin 13).

4. Connect the MAX31855 breakout board CS to the micro:bit pin 0.

5. Connect the MAX31855 breakout board D0 to the micro:bit MISO (pin 14).

Listing 4-6 shows the MicroPython code that reads the temperature through the SPI bus and then prints it in Celsius.

Listing 4-6. Reading Temperature Through an SPI Bus

```
from microbit import *

spi.init(baudrate=1000000, bits=8, mode=0, sclk=pin13,
mosi=pin15, miso=pin14)

def temp_c(data):
    temp = data[0] << 8 | data[1]
    if temp & 0x0001:
        return float('NaN')  # Fault reading data.
    temp >>= 2
    if temp & 0x2000:
        temp -= 16384  # Sign bit set, take 2's compliment.
    return temp * 0.25
```

```
while True:
    data = spi.read(4)
    print(temp_c(data))
    sleep(100)
```

The spi.init() function is used to initialize SPI communication with the specified parameters on the specified pins:

- baudrate: 1000000 (the speed of communication)

- bits: 8 (the number of bytes being transmitted)

- mode: 0

- sclk: Pin 13 (micro:bit pin 13 SCK)

- mosi: Pin 15 (optional, as you will be reading data through the SPI)

- miso: Pin 14 (micro:bit pin 14 MISO)

After initializing the SPI communication between both devices, the spi.read() function is used to read data from the MAX31855 sensor. The MAX31855 sensor has a very simple interface where you can read four bytes of data (32 bits total) to get the current temperature reading and other sensor states.

```
data = spi.read(4)
```

The helper function called temp_c() gets the temperature data from the 32-bit result. Finally, the print() function will print the temperature. A 100ms delay will be added between each temp_c() function call to give it enough time to get the temperature data from the data register.

UART (Universal Asynchronous Receiver-Transmitter)

micro:bit supports data communication with devices that have a UART (Universal Asynchronous Receiver Transmitter) interface. The MicroPython `uart` module allows you talk to a device connected to your board using a serial interface.

Devices with a UART interface have two pins (or wires) for transmitting and receiving data. Normally, these pins are called Tx (transmit) and Rx (receive).

The following example explains how to connect the micro:bit to a mini thermal receipt printer that has a UART interface.

To build the example project, you need the following things.

- Mini thermal receipt printer (`https://www.adafruit.com/product/597`)

- 5V 2A (2000mA) switching power supply (`https://www.adafruit.com/product/276`)

- Female DC power adapter, 2.1mm jack to screw terminal block (`https://www.adafruit.com/product/368`)

- Thermal paper roll that's 16 feet long, 2.25 inches (`https://www.adafruit.com/product/2755`)

- micro:bit

- A few crocodile clips and wires

The mini thermal receipt printer is ideal for interfacing with the micro:bit through the a UART interface. Figure 4-23 shows the wiring diagram between micro:bit and the printer.

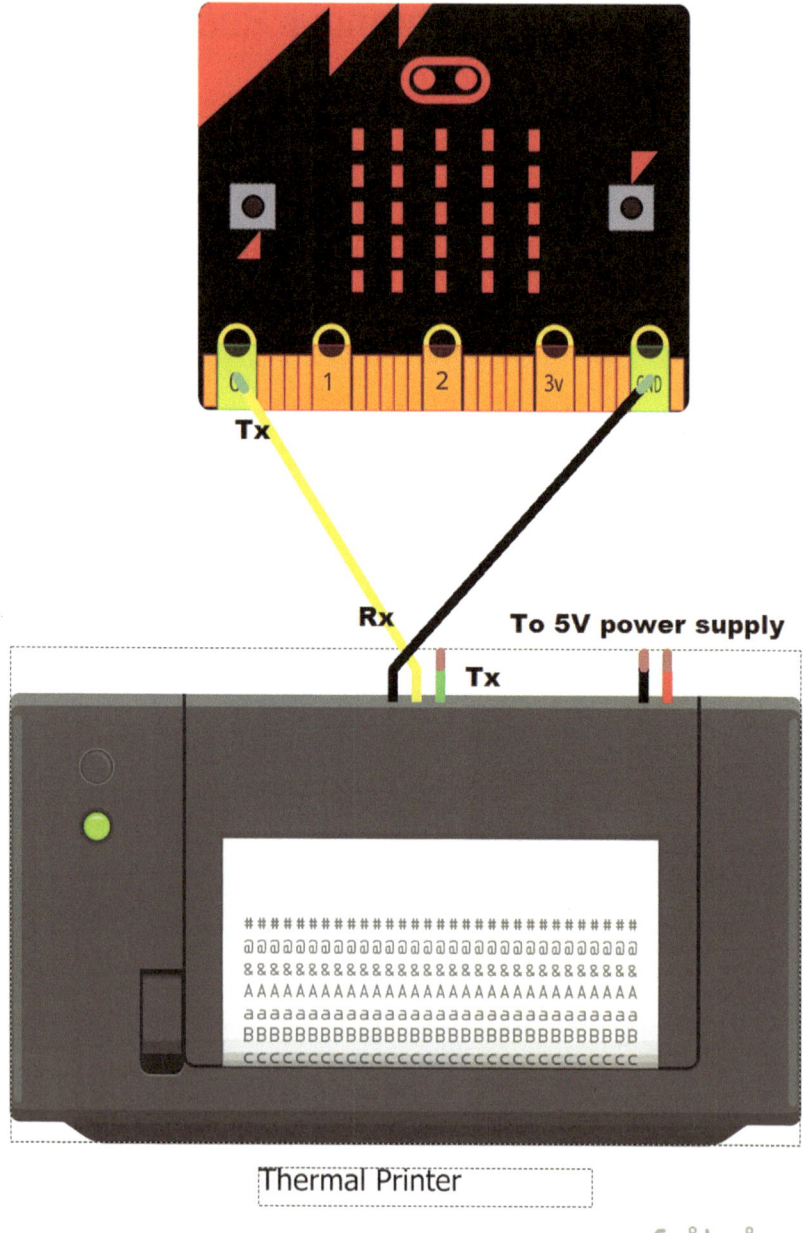

Figure 4-23. *Wiring diagram for UART communication*

The following steps guide you in how to connect the printer with micro:bit.

1. The back panel of the printer has two 3-pin connectors—one for power and one for serial communications.

2. First, connect the provided data cable to the printer. The data cable has three wires—black, yellow, and green.

    - Black = GND

    - Yellow = Data IN to the printer (RX)

    - Green = Data OUT of the printer (TX)

3. Connect the data cable to the micro:bit as shown in Figure 4-1.

    - Connect the black cable to the micro:bit GND

    - Connect the yellow cable to the micro:bit pin 0

4. Connect the power cable of the printer with the 5V 2A switching power supply through the female DC power adapter and apply power.

Listing 4-7 shows sample code that can be used to send text to the printer through UART for printing. Flash it to the micro:bit using the Mu editor.

Listing 4-7. Sending Text to the Printer

```
from microbit import *

uart.init(baudrate=19200, bits=8, parity=None, stop=1,tx=pin0)
```

```
while True:
    if button_a.was_pressed():
        uart.write('Button A was pressed\x0A\x0A')
    elif button_b.was_pressed():
        uart.write('Button B was pressed\x0A\x0A')
    sleep(100)
```

5. After flashing the code, simply press and release the
    built-in buttons A and B to test the code. The \x0A at
    the end of each message is a hex code for line feed.

6. The uart.init() function initializes serial
    communication with the specified parameters
    on the specified **tx** and **rx** pins. For correct
    communication, the parameters must be the
    same on both devices. The following is the list of
    parameters you can use.

    • baudrate: The speed of communication (9600, 14400,
      19200, 28800, 38400, 57600, or 115200). The thermal
      printer ships with a default of 19200bps baud rate.

      uart.init(**baudrate=9600**, bits=8, parity=None,
      stop=1,tx=pin0)

    • bits: Defines the size of bytes being transmitted.

      uart.init(baudrate=9600, **bits=8**, parity=None,
      stop=1,tx=pin0)

    • parity: Defines how parity is checked, and it can be
      None, microbit.uart.ODD, or microbit.uart.EVEN.

      uart.init(baudrate=9600, bits=8, **parity=None**,
      stop=1,tx=pin0)

- stop: The stop parameter tells the number of stop bits,
  and must be 1 for this board.

  ```
  uart.init(baudrate=9600, bits=8, parity=None,
  stop=1,tx=pin0)
  ```

- tx: This is the pin used to transmit data. Connect this
  pin to the RX pin of your UART device. The previous
  code used micro:bit pin 0 to connect to the RX pin of
  the printer.

  ```
  uart.init(baudrate=9600, bits=8, parity=None,
  stop=1,tx=pin0)
  ```

- rx: This is the pin used to receive data. Connect this
  pin to the TX pin of your UART device. The previous
  code only transmits data to the computer and is not for
  receiving, so you can ignore the **rx** parameter.

- The uart.write() function is used to write a buffer of
  bytes to the UART bus. You can input any text in to this
  function:

  ```
  uart.write('Button A was pressed\x0A\x0A')
  ```

Summary

In this chapter, you learned about the 21 I/O pins in the micro:bit edge
connector. Then you built some simple projects based on digital, analog,
touch, I2C, SPI, and UART to see how they work with the micro:bit.

In next chapter, you learn in-depth about the micro:bit built-in
accelerometer and compass (magnetometer).

CHAPTER 5

Using the Accelerometer and Compass

The micro:bit board comes with built-in accelerometer and a compass that allows you to build applications that respond to the acceleration and magnetic field of the earth.

In this chapter, you learn how to take readings from the built-in accelerometer and compass (magnetometer) to build applications using MicroPython.

Accelerometer

The micro:bit has an on-board NXP/Freescale MMA8652 chip (see Figure 5-1), which is a three-axis accelerometer that can be used to measure the acceleration. The accelerometer is internally connected to the micro:bit's I2C bus.

© Pradeeka Seneviratne 2018
P. Seneviratne, *Beginning BBC micro:bit*, https://doi.org/10.1007/978-1-4842-3360-3_5

Figure 5-1. *The micro:bit accelerometer*

Reading Acceleration

The accelerometer measures the acceleration or movement along the three axes (see Figure 5-2): x and y axes (the horizontal planes), and the z axis (the vertical plane), which it experiences relative to freefall. This is most commonly called the g-force. With the micro:bit's accelerometer, you will get acceleration values in mG (milliG).

> *1000mG = 1G*

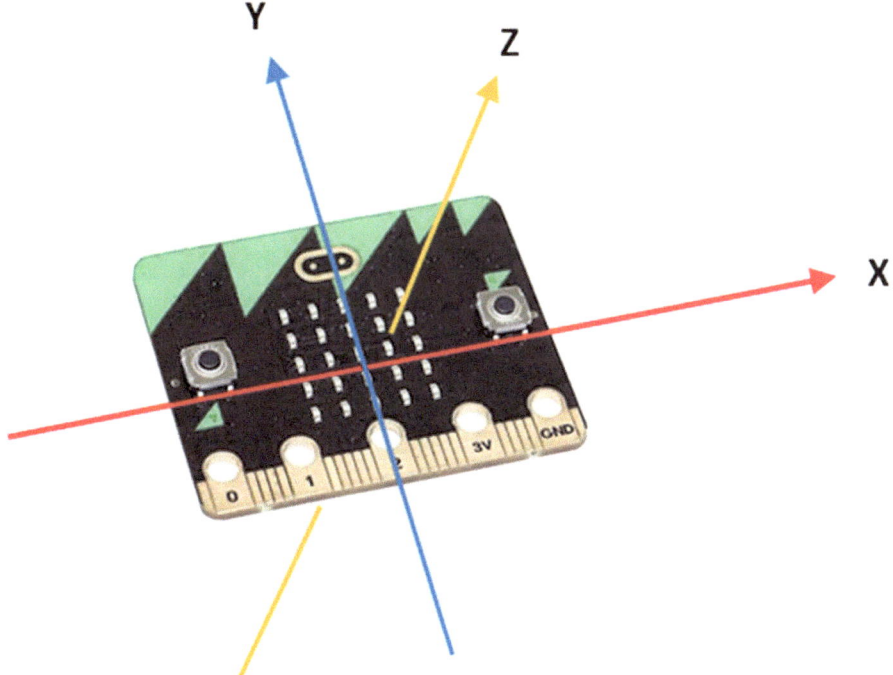

Figure 5-2. *Three axes of the accelerometer (Image source: micro:bit Foundation)*

When you place the micro:bit board on the surface of the earth, it will measure acceleration due to the earth's gravity, straight upward of g ≈ 9.81 m/s2. The micro:bit accelerometer can measure accelerations between +2g and -2g. This range is suitable to use with wide range of applications.

Listing 5-1 presents the MicroPython code that gets the values in mG for movement along three axes.

Listing 5-1. Reading Acceleration Along Three Axes

```
from microbit import *
while True:
    x = accelerometer.get_x()
    y = accelerometer.get_y()
    z = accelerometer.get_z()
    print("x, y, z:", x, y, z)
    sleep(500)
```

Type this code into the Mu editor and then click the Repl button followed by the Flash button to upload the code to the micro:bit. Hold the micro:bit board flat with the LEDs in the uppermost corner, without removing the USB cable.

You will get similar output as shown in Figure 5-3.

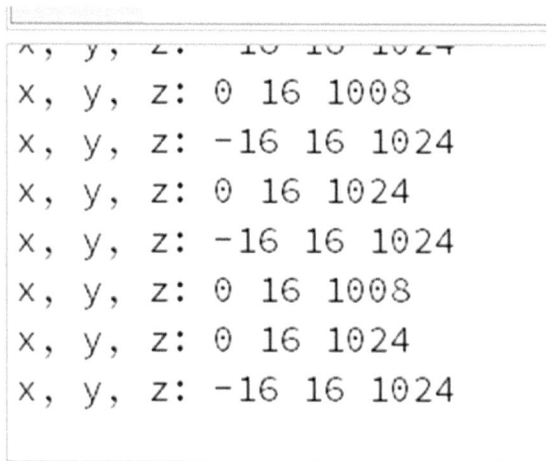

Figure 5-3. *Accelerometer readings for movement in the x, y, and z planes*

You can see that the acceleration values for x and y are close to 0 and the acceleration value for z axis is close to 1024. If you tilt the micro:bit slowly along the x axis, you can change the value to nearly 0. The value 0 indicates that your micro:bit board is in the spirit level. A similar technology is used in electronic spirit levels to detect the horizontal level with the x and y axes.

The same result can be achieved with the `accelerometer.get_values()` function. It outputs the acceleration values of the x, y, and z axes as a three-element tuple of integers.

Note   A *tuple* is a sequence of immutable Python objects. Tuples act just like lists, but the elements of a tuple cannot be changed once they have been assigned. Tuples use parentheses to hold objects. You can also store different types of objects in a tuple.

tuple = ([1,2], (3,4), "micropython", 2017)

Listing 5-2 shows the same implementation of code that reads the acceleration values along the three axes.

Listing 5-2. Reading Acceleration Along Three Axes as a Tuple

```
from microbit import *
while True:
    result = accelerometer.get_values()
    print("Values:", result)
    sleep(500)
```

Figure 5-4 shows the output for this code when you hold the micro:bit flat with the LEDs at the top.

```
Values: (80, 96, 1024)
Values: (112, 80, -1024)
Values: (112, 80, -1040)
Values: (80, 96, -1024)
Values: (-112, 176, -1328)
Values: (-80, 0, -1040)
Values: (48, -16, -1120)
Values: (32, 0, -1008)
Values: (48, 0, -1040)
Values: (64, 0, -1024)
Values: (64, 0, -1088)
Values: (32, 0, -992)
Values: (32, 0, -1024)
Values: (48, -16, -1024)
Values: (48, 0, -1024)
```

Figure 5-4. *Reading acceleration along three axes*

Building a Spirit Level

A spirit level, bubble level, or simply a *level,* is an instrument designed to indicate whether a surface is horizontal (level) along the x axis. Different types of spirit levels may be used by carpenters, stonemasons, bricklayers, other building trades workers, surveyors, millwrights, and other metalworkers, as well as in some photographic or videographic work.

Listing 5-3 shows an example of how to code a simple spirit level.

Listing 5-3. Simple Spirit Level

```python
from microbit import *

while True:
    val = accelerometer.get_x()
    if val > 0:
```

```
        display.show(Image.ARROW_W)
    elif val < 0:
        display.show(Image.ARROW_E)
    else:
        display.show(Image.YES)
```

This code will show the YES image (tick mark) when it detects the spirit level. Otherwise, it will show the left arrow or right arrow so you can tilt the micro:bit to get the spirit level.

Calculating Overall Acceleration

The overall acceleration can be calculated with the Pythagorean Theorem, as shown here. The formula uses the acceleration along the x and y axes to calculate the overall acceleration.

$$acceleration = \sqrt{x^2 + y^2}$$

If you want, you can calculate the overall acceleration along the x, y, and z axes.

$$acceleration = \sqrt{x^2 + y^2 + z^2}$$

Listing 5-4 shows the MicroPython code to calculate the overall acceleration in milliG with the acceleration values of all three axes.

Listing 5-4. Calculating Overall Acceleration with x, y, and z Values

```
from microbit import *
import math

while True:
    x = accelerometer.get_x()
```

```
y = accelerometer.get_y()
z = accelerometer.get_z()
acceleration = math.sqrt(x**2 + y**2 + z**2)
print("acceleration", acceleration)
sleep(500)
```

Figure 5-5 shows the overall acceleration when you move the micro:bit board.

```
acceleration 2904.518
acceleration 1221.356
acceleration 1164.927
acceleration 1028.241
acceleration 1059.147
acceleration 847.396
acceleration 1010.41
acceleration 955.4558
acceleration 1068.651
acceleration 1022.749
acceleration 1022.749
acceleration 1022.749
```

Figure 5-5. *Overall acceleration*

Gesture Detection

The micro:bit's built-in accelerometer can also be used to create interactive applications based on gestures. The following gestures are recognized by the micro:bit.

- Up

- Down

- Left

- Right

- Face up

- Face down

- Freefall

- Shake

Figure 5-6 shows how you can perform these gestures by holding the micro:bit in your hand.

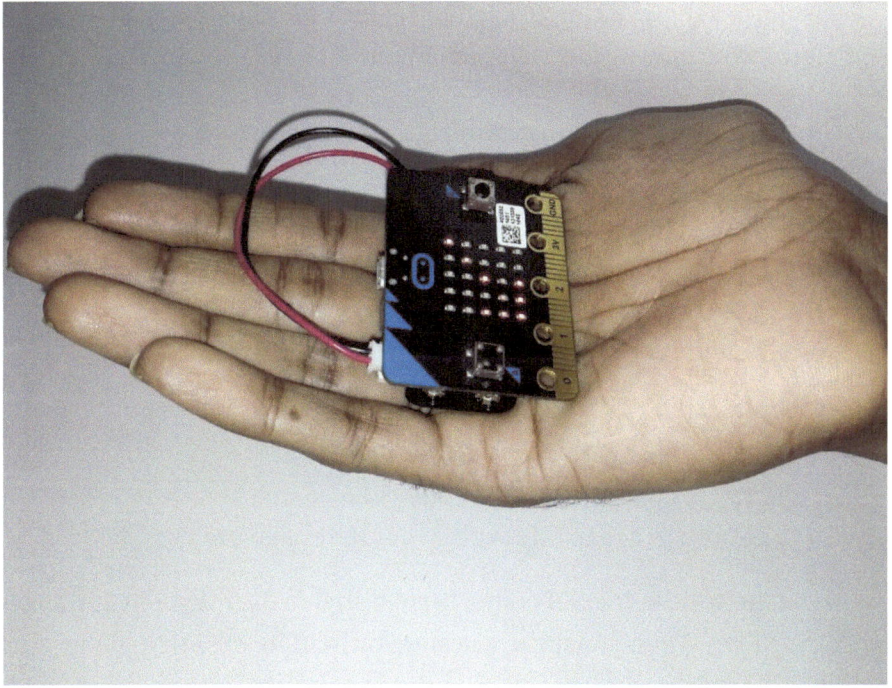

Figure 5-6. *Performing gestures with micro:bit (i.e., UP)*

In addition to these basic gestures, you can also detect some advanced gestures with the micro:bit related to the gravitational forces. They are:

- 2G

- 4G

- 8G

Detecting the Current Gesture

The MicroPython provides some useful functions that you can use with the accelerometer to work with gesture detection.

Listing 5-5 shows a simple example of how MicroPython can be used to detect the current gesture with micro:bit.

Listing 5-5. Detecting and Printing Current Gesture

```
from microbit import *

last_gesture = ""

while True:
    current_gesture = accelerometer.current_gesture()
    sleep(100)
    if current_gesture is not last_gesture:
        last_gesture = current_gesture
        print('>{g:s}<'.format(g=current_gesture))
```

Type the code in the Mu editor, then flash it to the micro:bit and run with the REPL. When you make a gesture by holding the micro:bit in your hand, the terminal window will print the name of the detected gestures, as shown in Figure 5-7. The last gesture you performed can be found at the end of the list.

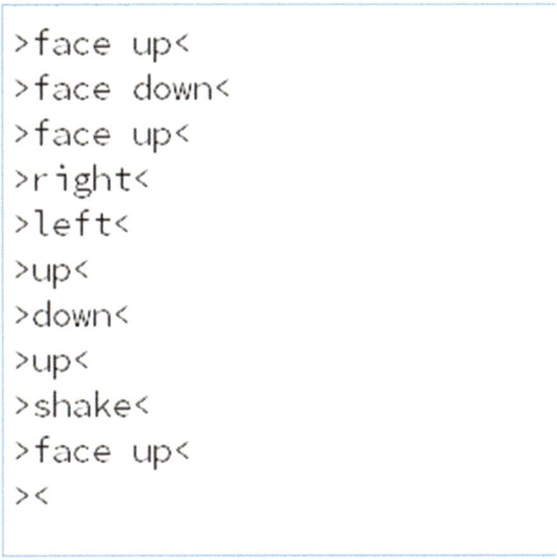

```
>face up<
>face down<
>face up<
>right<
>left<
>up<
>down<
>up<
>shake<
>face up<
><
```

Figure 5-7. *Output shows the current gesture*

The accelerometer.current_gesture() function returns the name of the current gesture as a string. Listing 5-6 lists the valid names for each gesture that you can use with MicroPython. When you perform a new gesture, the accelerometer.current_gesture() function stores this value in current_gesture. If last_gesture is different, it is updated to this new value and the gesture name is printed on the REPL screen.

Listing 5-6. Valid Gesture Names

```
up
down
left
right
face up
face down
freefall
shake
```

3g

6g

8g

Listing 5-7 shows the MicroPython code that can be used to detect the "face up" gesture. If it detects the "face up" gesture, a HAPPY image will display on the LED screen; otherwise, it will display an ANGRY image. The accelerometer.current_gesture() function returns the name of the gesture that you performed. Then it compares the returned gesture name with the "face up" string. If both are equal, a HAPPY face will display on the LED screen; otherwise, the screen will display a SAD image.

Listing 5-7. Detecting a "Face Up" Gesture

```
from microbit import *

while True:
    gesture = accelerometer.current_gesture()
    if gesture == "face up":
        display.show(Image.HAPPY)
    else:
        display.show(Image.ANGRY)
```

This code can be rewritten using the accelerometer.is_gesture(name) function for the same application, as shown in Listing 5-8.

Listing 5-8. Detecting a "Face Up" Gesture

```
from microbit import *

while True:
    if accelerometer.is_gesture("face up"):
        display.show(Image.HAPPY)
    else:
        display.show(Image.ANGRY)
```

The accelerometer.is_gesture(name) function returns true if the given gesture is currently active; otherwise, it returns false.

If you want to get a gesture after it is completed by the user, accelerometer.was_gesture(name) can be used. Listing 5-9 shows example code to get the previous gesture.

Listing 5-9. Detect Whether the micro:bit Has Been Shook

```
from microbit import *
while True:
    display.show('8')
    if accelerometer.was_gesture('shake'):
        display.clear()
        sleep(1000)
        display.scroll("shaked")
    sleep(10)
```

Getting Gesture History

You can get the gesture history with the accelerometer.get_gestures() function, as shown in Listing 5-10. It returns a tuple of the gesture history. The most recent gesture is listed last in the tuple.

Listing 5-10. Getting Gesture History

```
from microbit import *

gestList = []
while True:

    gestures = accelerometer.get_gestures()

    print(len(gestures))

    if len(gestures) == 1:
```

```
        gestList.append(gestures[0])
        sleep(500)

    print("History: "+str(gestList))
```

Using the Mu editor, type and flash this code to the micro:bit. Then open the REPL interactive shell and perform some gestures by holding the micro:bit with your hand. You will get the output shown in Figure 5-8.

```
History: ['down', 'left', 'freefall', 'freefall', 'freefall', 'freefall']
0
History: ['down', 'left', 'freefall', 'freefall', 'freefall', 'freefall']
0
History: ['down', 'left', 'freefall', 'freefall', 'freefall', 'freefall']
1
l', 'freefall', 'freefall', 'freefall']
0
History: ['down', 'left', 'freefall', 'freefall', 'freefall', 'freefall']
0
History: ['down', 'left', 'freefall', 'freefall', 'freefall', 'freefall']
0
History: ['down', 'left', 'freefall', 'freefall', 'freefall', 'freefall']
0
```

Figure 5-8. *Gesture history*

Note   There may be a bug in the get_gestures() method and you can't get the output you expected in the program. When you start a REPL session with the code in Listing 5-10, the Mu editor may sometimes appear to be frozen or non-responsive.

Compass

Micro:bit comes with a built-in compass based on the NXP/Freescale MAG3110, which is three-axis *magnetometer* sensor that can be accessed via the I2C bus. The compass can also act as a metal detector. Figure 5-9 shows the NXP/Freescale MAG3110 chip, which you'll see on the back of the micro:bit board.

Figure 5-9. *The micro:bit compass*

Calibrating the Compass

Before using the compass, you should calibrate it to ensure correct readings. It's also wise to calibrate the compass each time you use it in a new location.

In some situations, when the compass needs to be calibrated, the micro:bit will automatically prompt the user to calibrate it. However, the calibration sequence can also be manually started with the compass. calibrate() function.

To calibrate the compass, tilt the micro:bit around until a circle of pixels is drawn on the outside edges of the display.

Figure 5-10 shows the process of calibrating the micro:bit compass. After calibrating the compass successfully, the micro:bit display will show a smiley face on the LED display.

Figure 5-10. *Calibrating the micro:bit compass*

Reading Compass Values

When you want to determine the direction using the micro:bit compass, you will only need to measure the magnetic field strength in the x and y axes. Figure 5-11 shows the three axes—x, y, and z—that you can use to get the strength of the magnetic field.

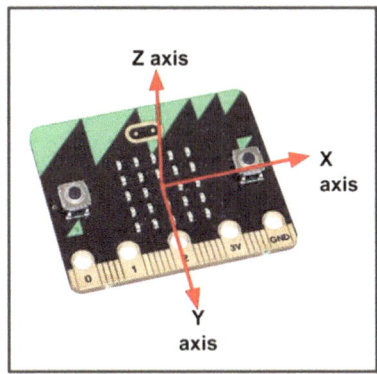

Figure 5-11. *Compass reading for three axes*

Listing 5-11 shows the sample code that can be used to read the strength of the magnetic field in the x and y axes. The `compass.get_y()` and `compass.get_x()` functions return magnetic field strength in the x and y axes.

Listing 5-11. Reading the Strength of the Magnetic Field in the x and y Axes

```
from microbit import *

compass.calibrate()

while True:
    x = compass.get_x()
    y = compass.get_y()
    print("x reading: ", x, ", y reading: ", y)
    sleep(500)
```

Figure 5-12 shows the output for this code when it's run with the Mu. As you can see, the stronger magnetic fields are represented by bigger values.

```
x reading:   43728 , y reading:   9873
x reading:   37828 , y reading:  -23127
x reading:   30628 , y reading:  -30627
x reading:   33128 , y reading:  -28127
x reading:   41228 , y reading:  -9727
x reading:   42928 , y reading:   4473
x reading:   43528 , y reading:   4273
x reading:   41528 , y reading:   15473
x reading:   39128 , y reading:   20873
x reading:   39528 , y reading:   21473
x reading:   39528 , y reading:   20673
x reading:   39428 , y reading:   21273
x reading:   39128 , y reading:   21173
x reading:   39228 , y reading:   21273
```

Figure 5-12. *Magnetic field in x and y axes*

Getting Compass Heading

The compass heading represents an angle in the number of degrees from the north, moving clockwise, which ranges from 0 to 360. North is set to 0. For an example, the compass heading 45 degrees represents the direction of west.

The magnetic field in the x and y axes of the micro:bit compass can be used to calculate the compass heading value using the following formula.

1. First, calculate the arc tangent using x and y values
    with the math.atan2() function. You will get the
    result in radians.

```
Arc tangent = math.atan2(y,x)
```

2. Then convert radians into degrees by multiplying it
    with 180/Pi.

```
Angle in degrees (compass heading) = math.
atan2(y,x) *180/math.pi
```

Listing 5-12 shows sample code that can be used to calculate the
compass heading with x and y values. The same code can be found at
`http://microbit-challenges.readthedocs.io/en/latest/tutorials/`
`compass.html` and is used in this book to demonstrate the output.

Listing 5-12. Calculate the Compass Heading Using x and y Values

```python
import math
from microbit import *

compass.calibrate()

while True:
    x = compass.get_x()
    y = compass.get_y()
    angle = math.atan2(y,x) *180/math.pi
    print("x", x, " y", y)
    print("Direction: ", angle)
    sleep(500)
```

Figure 5-13 shows the output for this code. It shows the magnetic field
in x and y axes, and the calculated compass heading (direction) in degrees.

```
Direction:    70.7121
x 6886   y 38607
Direction:    79.88699
x 4086   y 35507
Direction:    83.43552
x 86    y 30507
Direction:    89.83848
x 2786   y 32807
Direction:    85.14603
x 986    y 30307
Direction:    88.1366
x -214   y 30107
Direction:    90.4072
x -314   y 28807
Direction:    90.62449
```

Figure 5-13. *Output of the x and y axes and the compass heading*

However, with MicroPython, you can use the compass.heading() function to easily get the compass heading in degrees from 0 to 360.

Note   The compass-heading function returns -1004 when the compass needs to be calibrated.

Listing 5-13 shows simple code that can be used to read the compass heading.

Listing 5-13. Reading the Compass Heading

```python
from microbit import *

compass.calibrate()

while True:
    heading = compass.heading()
    print("heading: ", heading)
    sleep(500)
```

Figure 5-14 shows the output of Listing 5-13 when you run it with the Mu.

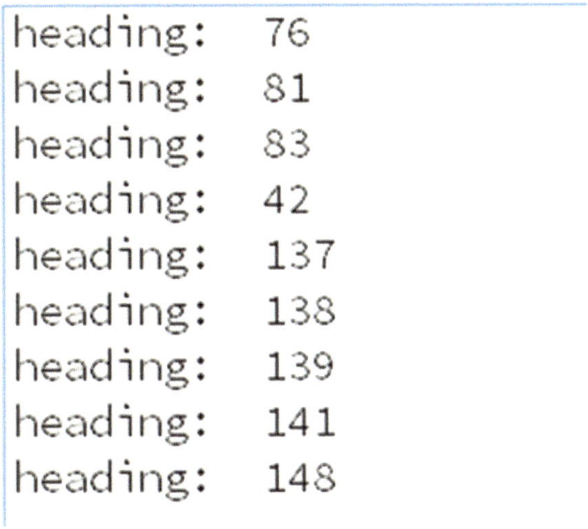

```
heading:    76
heading:    81
heading:    83
heading:    42
heading:    137
heading:    138
heading:    139
heading:    141
heading:    148
```

Figure 5-14. *Compass heading values in degrees*

You can modify this code to show the bearing to north on the micro:bit display. Listing 5-14 shows the sample micro:bit code that can be used to display the compass heading with the ALL_CLOCKS image list.

Listing 5-14. Displaying the Compass Heading

```
from microbit import *

compass.calibrate()

while True:
    sleep(100)
    needle = ((15 - compass.heading()) // 30) % 12
    display.show(Image.ALL_CLOCKS[needle])
```

This code displays the compass heading (see Figure 5-15) on the micro:bit display and updates it when you rotate the micro:bit board.

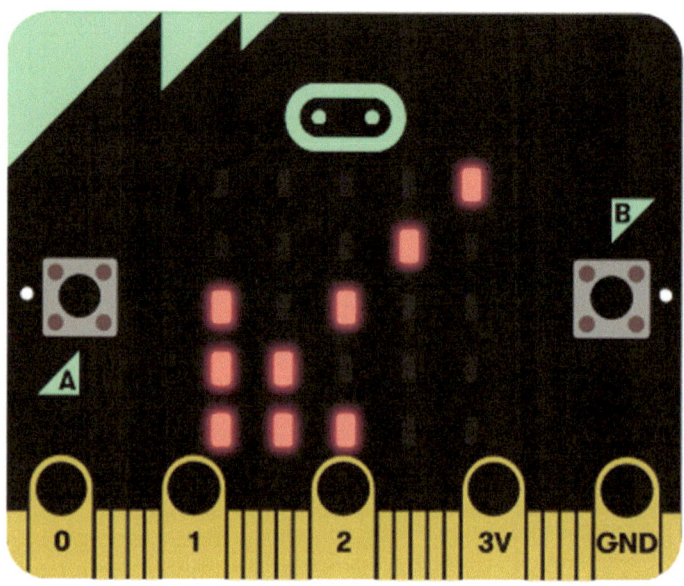

Figure 5-15. *Compass heading to southwest*

Summary

In this chapter, you built several applications with the micro:bit accelerometer and the compass. The gesture detection is one of the most interesting features of MicroPython, in conjunction with the accelerometer.

In next chapter, you learn how to connect a speaker and write applications with micro:bit's music library to make melodies.

CHAPTER 6

Working with Music

In this chapter, you learn how to use the micro:bit music library to build and play simple tunes. The music library allows you to build music by combining music notes, octaves, beats (duration), accidentals (flats and sharps), and so forth. You can also use built-in melodies in your applications.

By default, the music module expects the speaker to be connected through micro:bit's pin 0. However, you can use any analog pin to connect the speaker (or multiple speakers) by defining the output pin to override the default pin 0.

Connecting a Speaker

You can connect a speaker to the micro:bit pin 0 through the edge connector. An 8-ohm speaker is ideal to work with micro:bit to produce audio. Figure 6-1 shows a small 8-ohm speaker (`https://www.kitronik.co.uk/3341-thin-speaker.html`) that can be used with the micro:bit.

© Pradeeka Seneviratne 2018
P. Seneviratne, *Beginning BBC micro:bit*, https://doi.org/10.1007/978-1-4842-3360-3_6

Figure 6-1. *0.25W 8-ohm 40mm thin speaker front and rear views (image courtesy of Kitronik at* `https://www.kitronik.co.uk`*)*

A speaker has two wires, positive (red) and negative (black). Some speakers use different colored codes for positive and negative leads. With some speakers, you must solder wires to the solder tabs before using them. Figure 6-2 shows how to wire the speaker with the micro:bit using the edge connector breakout board. The speaker doesn't use a separate power line and gets the power from pin 0.

1. Connect the positive lead of the speaker to the micro:bit pin 0.

2. Connect the negative lead of the speaker to the micro:bit GND.

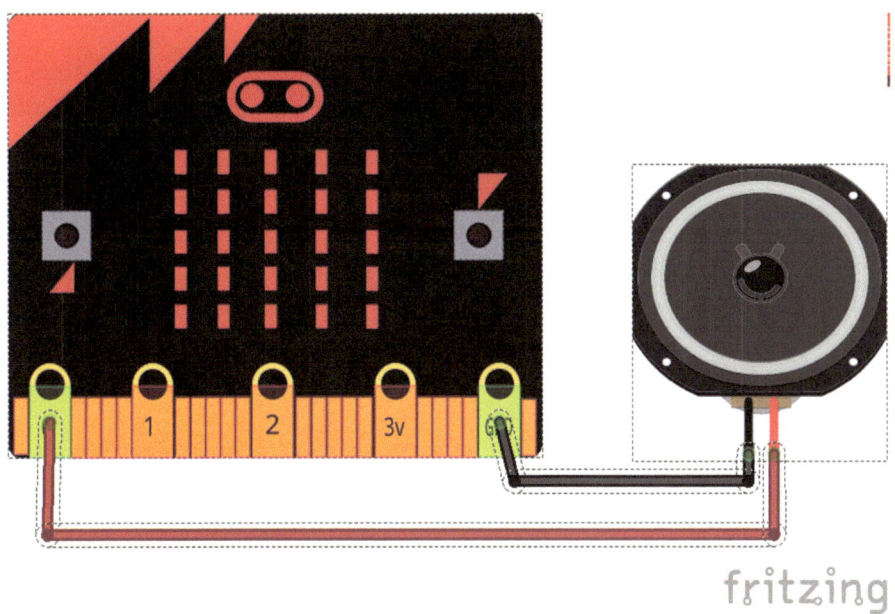

Figure 6-2. *Wiring between the micro:bit and a speaker*

Simply use crocodile leads (`https://www.kitronik.co.uk/2407-crocodile-leads-pack-of-10.html`) to make these connections (see Figure 6-3).

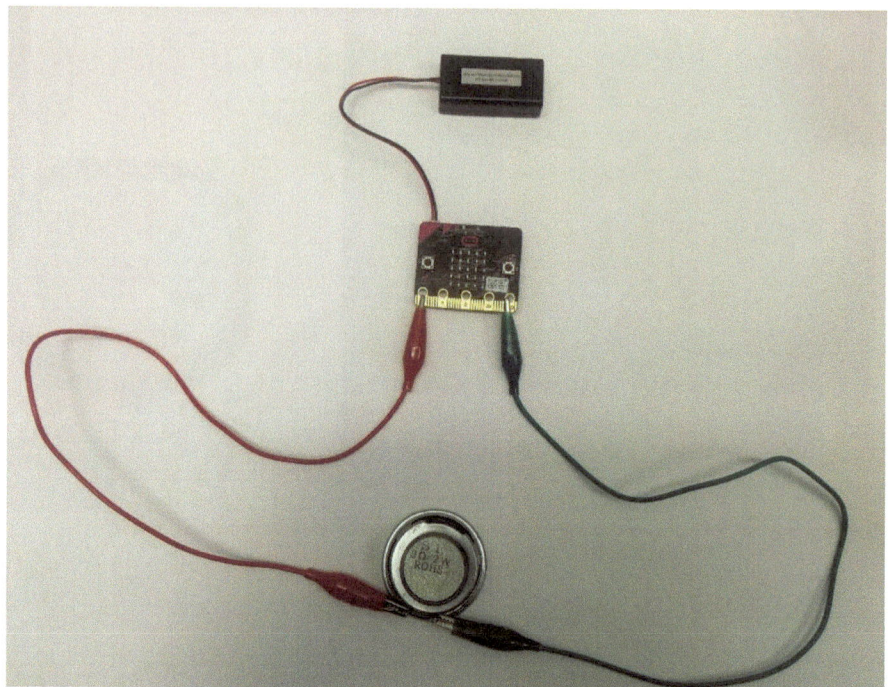

Figure 6-3. *Wiring between micro:bit and a speaker with crocodile leads (Image credits:* `http://learnlearn.uk/microbit/`*)*

When attaching the crocodile clips to the micro:bit, make sure that the clips are perpendicular to the board so that they are not touching any of the neighboring connectors on the micro:bit edge connector (see Figure 6-4).

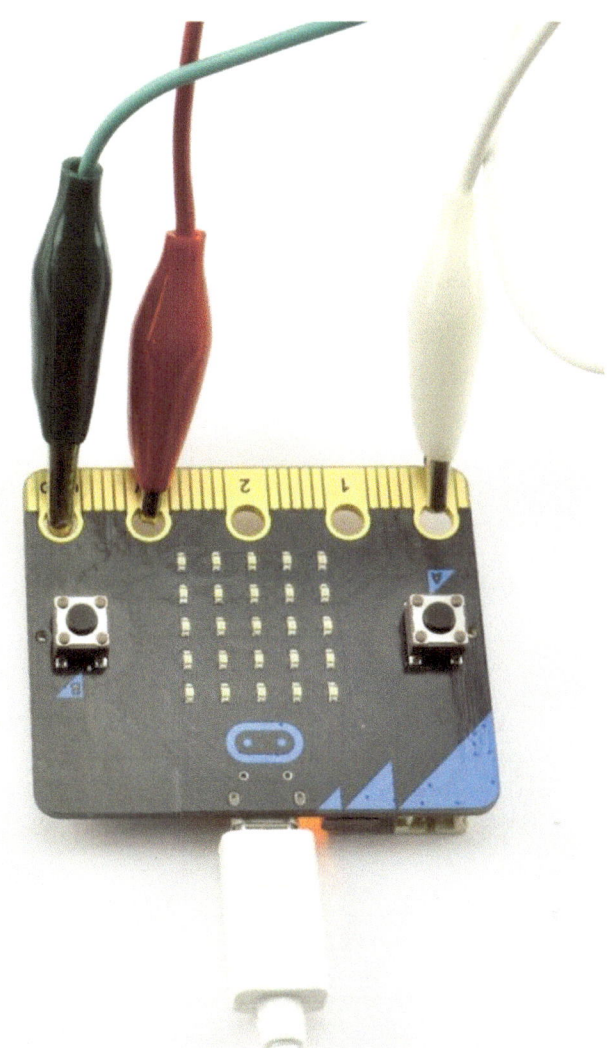

Figure 6-4. *Attaching crocodile clips perpendicular to the board bit (image credit: Monk Makes at* `https://www.monkmakes.com/`*)*

Alternatively, you can use an edge connector breakout board to make the setup neater, as shown in Figure 6-5. You will need following components in addition to build the setup.

- Edge connector breakout

- Breadboard

- Male/female jumper wires (https://www.kitronik. co.uk/4129-jumper-wires-premium-mf-pack-of-10. html)

Figure 6-5. *Attaching crocodile clips perpendicular to the board (image courtesy of Kitronik at* https://www.kitronik.co.uk*)*

You cannot control the volume of the sound from the micro:bit. However, you can control the volume by adding a potentiometer (a volume control) to the micro:bit, as shown in the Figure 6-6.

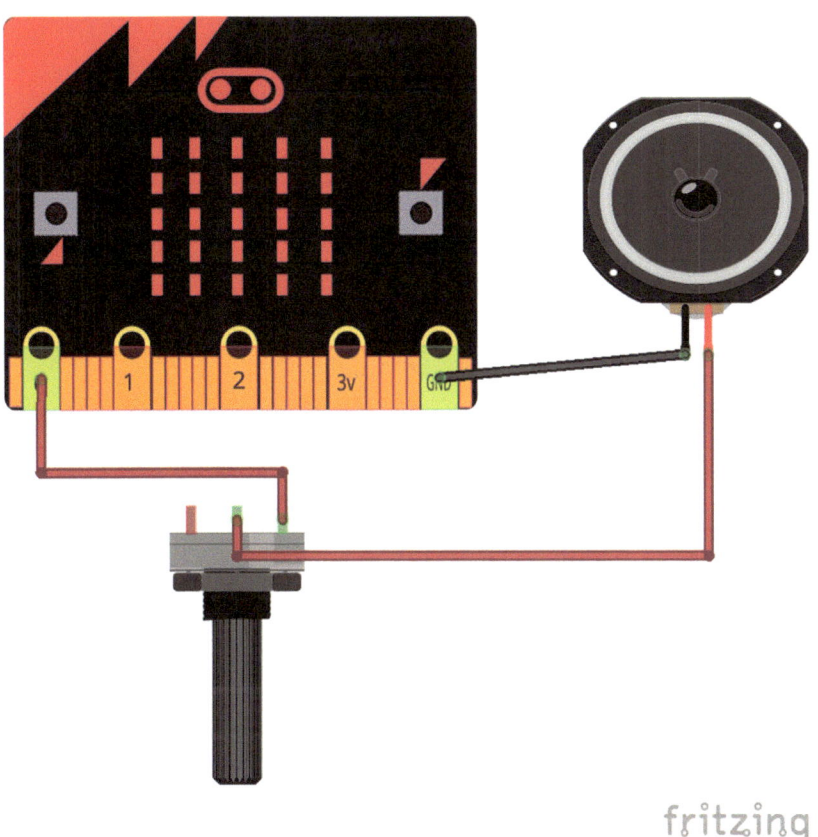

Figure 6-6. *Adding a potentiometer to the micro:bit to control the volume*

Some vendors offer speakers with built-in amplifiers to make louder music. If you need one, Monk Makes sells a speaker with a built-in amplifier for micro:bit (`https://www.monkmakes.com/mb_speaker/`). You can connect it to your micro:bit using alligator clips. As shown in Figure 6-7, it uses three wires for connectivity and draws additional power from the micro:bit's 3V pin. Table 6-1 shows the pin connection between the two boards.

Table 6-1. *Wiring Between Monk Makes Speakers and micro:bit*

Speaker	micro:bit
IN	pin 0
3V	3V
GND	GND

Figure 6-7. *Monk Makes speaker for micro:bit (image credit: Monk Makes at* `https://www.monkmakes.com/`*)*

If you want to play sound through more than one speaker, it is possible to connect multiple speakers to the micro:bit through different analog pins. However, you must carefully define the output pin for each speaker in the code.

Using Earphones

If you don't have a speaker, you can still use your micro:bit with earphones. You can connect earphones by cutting off the earphone jack and connecting the leads to the micro:bit GND and pin 0.

You can also use crocodile clips to connect a speaker to the micro:bit without cutting off the jack. The following list explains and Figure 6-8 shows how to connect crocodile clips to an earphone jack.

1. Take two crocodile leads (black and red).

2. Connect one end of the black crocodile lead to the micro:bit GND and the other end to the *base* of your earphone jack.

3. Connect one end of the red crocodile lead to the micro:bit pin 0 and the other end to the *tip* of the earphone jack.

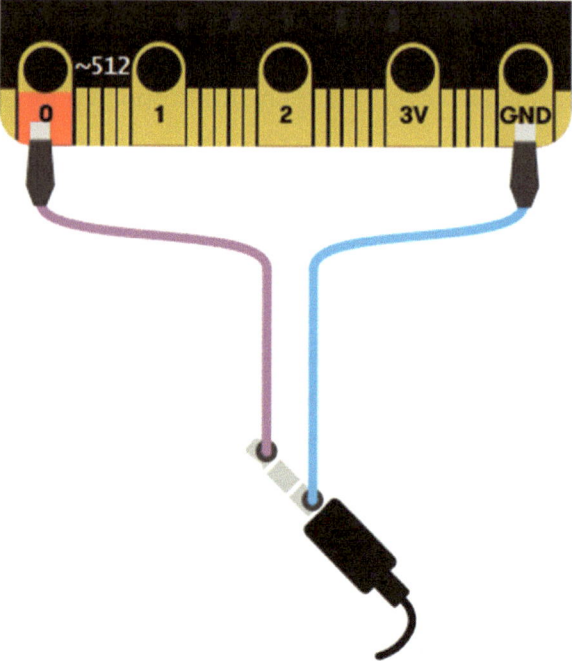

Figure 6-8. *Connecting an earphone to the micro:bit*

However, pre-built audio cables are available to quickly connect earphones or headphones to the micro:bit. Figure 6-9 shows an audio cable with a 3.5mm socket and two crocodile clips. You can simply connect the earphone jack to the 3.5mm socket of the audio cable and two crocodile clips to the micro:bit.

Figure 6-9. *Audio cable for micro:bit (image courtesy of Kitronik:* `https://www.kitronik.co.uk/5622-audio-cable-for-bbc-microbit.html`*)*

Built-in Melodies

The easiest way to get started with the micro:bit music library is using built-in melodies. It provides a set of built-in melodies that you can play with a simple MicroPython code.

The following list shows some interesting built-in melodies that you can use to play music. (Source: `http://microbit-micropython.readthedocs.io/en/latest/music.html`.)

- DADADADUM: The opening to Beethoven's 5th Symphony in C minor.

- ENTERTAINER: The opening fragment of Scott Joplin's Ragtime classic "The Entertainer".

- PRELUDE: The opening of the first Prelude in C major of J. S. Bach's 48 Preludes and Fugues.

- ODE: The "Ode to Joy" theme from Beethoven's 9th Symphony in D minor.

- NYAN: The Nyan Cat theme (`http://www.nyan.cat/`). The composer is unknown. This is fair use for educational purposes.

- RINGTONE: Something that sounds like a mobile phone ringtone. Used to indicate an incoming message.

- FUNK: A funky bass line for secret agents and criminal masterminds.

- BLUES: A boogie-woogie 12-bar blues walking bass.

- BIRTHDAY: "Happy Birthday to You…". For copyright status, see `http://www.bbc.co.uk/news/world-us-canada-34332853`.

- WEDDING: The bridal chorus from Wagner's opera "Lohengrin".

- FUNERAL: The "funeral march," otherwise known as Frédéric Chopin's Piano Sonata No. 2 in B minor, Op. 35.

- PUNCHLINE: A fun fragment that signifies a joke has been made.

- PYTHON: John Philip Sousa's march "Liberty Bell". The theme from "Monty Python's Flying Circus" (after which the Python programming language is named).

- BADDY: Silent movie era entrance of a bad guy.

- CHASE: Silent movie era chase scene.

- BA_DING: A short signal to indicate something has happened.

- WAWAWAWAA: A very sad trombone.

- JUMP_UP: For use in a game, indicating upward movement.

- JUMP_DOWN: For use in a game, indicating downward movement.

- POWER_UP: A fanfare to indicate an achievement has been unlocked.

- POWER_DOWN: A sad fanfare to indicate an achievement has been lost.

Let's write simple MicroPython code to play the melody BIRTHDAY. Listing 6-1 shows the complete MicroPython code.

Listing 6-1. Playing a Melody

```
from microbit import *
import music

music.play(music.BIRTHDAY)
```

The second line of the code imports the music library from MicroPython. Then it plays the "Happy Birthday to You…" built-in melody by using the music.play() function. You must provide the name of the melody (i.e., BIRTHDAY) as the input. You can modify the code with different melody names.

You can play a melody continuously by adding the loop=True keyword as shown in Listing 6-2.

Listing 6-2. Playing a Melody Continuously

```
from microbit import *
import music

music.play(music.BIRTHDAY, loop=True)
```

By default, the music module expects the speaker to be connected via pin 0. If you want to connect the speaker to a different pin, let's say to pin 1 (see Figure 6-10), write the code shown in Listing 6-3.

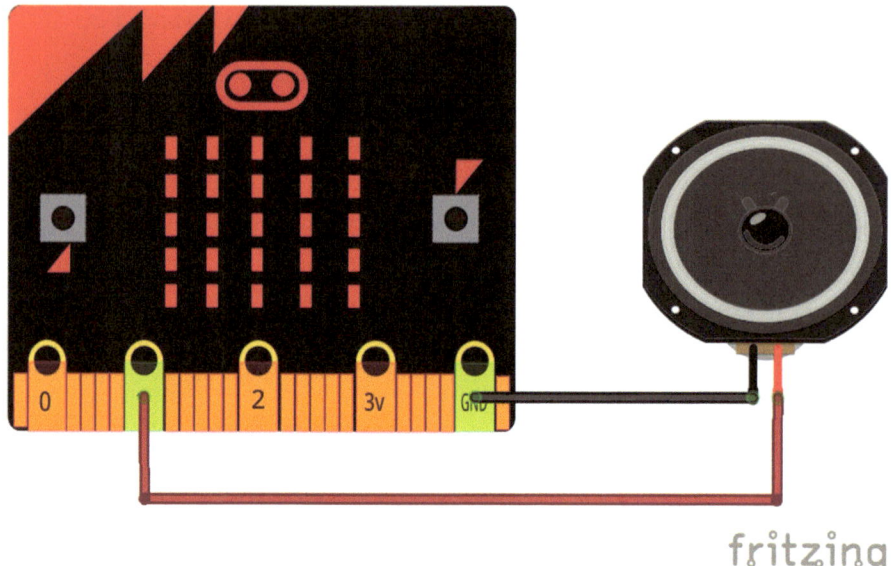

Figure 6-10. *Connecting speaker to pin 1*

Listing 6-3. Playing a Melody by Connecting a Speaker to Pin 1

```
from microbit import *
import music

music.play(music.BIRTHDAY, pin=pin1, loop=True)
```

Making Your Own Melodies

In music, a note is the pitch and duration of a sound. The following are the basic notes used with English music.

C, D, E, E, F, G, A, B

In Neo-Latin music, the same thing can be written as follows.

Do, Re, Me, Fa, Sol, La, Si

With MicroPython, you can easily play a musical note or a set of notes in a sequence.

Let's start with a single note. Listing 6-4 shows the MicroPython code to play the musical note C. With this code, you can press built-in button A on the micro:bit board to play the note. Before running your code with the micro:bit, connect the crocodile clip back to pin 0.

Listing 6-4. Playing a Single Musical Note

```
from microbit import *
import music

while True:
 if button_a.is_pressed():
  # Play a 'C'
  music.play('C')
```

You can also play many musical notes sequentially to make melodies. The code shown in Listing 6-5 plays the five basic musical notes.

Listing 6-5. Playing Musical Notes

```
from microbit import *
import music

while True:
 if button_a.is_pressed():
  # Play a 'C'
  music.play('C')
  # Play a 'D'
  music.play('D')
  # Play a 'E'
  music.play('E')
  # Play a 'F'
  music.play('F')
  # Play a 'G'
  music.play('G')
```

```
# Play a 'A'
music.play('A')
# Play a 'B'
music.play('B')
```

The code in Listing 6-5 can also be written with a few lines of code to produce the same output, as shown in Listing 6-6.

Listing 6-6. Playing Musical Notes

```
from microbit import *

import music
tune = ["C", "D", "E", "F", "G"]
music.play(tune)
```

You can use the note name R to create silence in your melody. For an example, the code in Listing 6-7 will add silence between the musical notes E and F.

Listing 6-7. Adding Silence

```
from microbit import *

import music
tune = ["C", "D", "E", "R", "F", "G"]
music.play(tune)
```

Using Octave

In music, an octave or perfect octave is the interval between one musical pitch and another with half or double its frequency. Figure 6-11 shows a keyboard with four octaves, from octave 2 to octave 5.

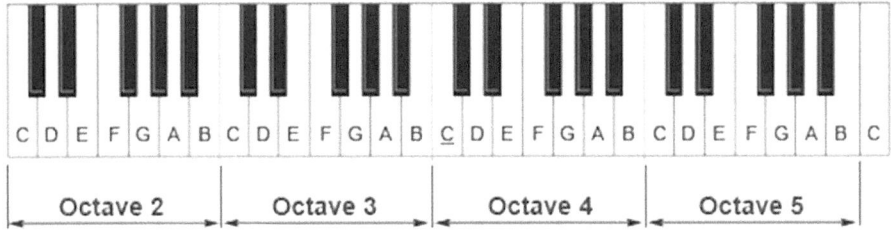

Figure 6-11. *Keyboard with four octaves*

Each octave has seven musical notes and they can be written with the letter followed by the number of the octave.

As an example, the musical note C belongs to octave 3 and can be written as C3.

Listing 6-8 shows code that plays the musical note C in octave 4.

Listing 6-8. Playing a Musical Note with Octave

```
from microbit import *
import music

while True:
 if button_a.is_pressed():
  # Play a 'C3'
  music.play('C3')
```

By default micro:bit plays musical notes in octave 4, unless you explicitly define it followed by the musical note. In other words, the musical note C is exactly equivalent to C4.

In addition to the octaves, accidentals (flats and sharps) can be denoted with musical notes. A flat is written as a lowercase *b* and a sharp is written as #. Listing 6-9 plays A flat and C sharp.

Listing 6-9. Playing Musical Notes with Accidentals

```
from microbit import *
import music

while True:
        if button_a.is_pressed():
        # Play a 'A-flat'
        music.play('Ab')
        # Play a 'C-sharp'
        music.play('C#')
```

Note   The default status of an octave is 4. As an example, if you write the musical note C in your code, it explicitly becomes C4.

Beats

In music, a beat is the basic unit of time. You can specify a musical note with a beat as follows:

NOTE[octave][:duration]

The duration specifies the arbitrary length of time defined by a tempo setting function (see the section called "Setting the Tempo").

If you want to play the musical note C in octave 4 for three beats, you can write it with the MicroPython shown in Listing 6-10.

Listing 6-10. Playing Musical Notes with Beats

```
from microbit import *
import music

while True:
        if button_a.is_pressed():
        # Play a 'C4:3'
        music.play('C4:3')
```

By default, micro:bit plays musical notes with four beats long unless you explicitly define the number of beats.

Setting the Tempo

The music.set_tempo() function makes the tempo (the speed of a piece of music) as fast or as slow as you say. With this function, you can set the number of ticks that constitute a beat. Each beat is played at a certain frequency per minute expressed as the more familiar bpm (beats per minute). Let's look at a few examples of how you can set the tempo with different parameters.

If you only need to change the definition of a beat, input the number of ticks that you want to define the beat with the music.set_tempo() function (see Listing 6-11).

Listing 6-11. Defining Number of Ticks

```
from microbit import *
import music

music.set_tempo(ticks=8) # set ticks to 8
music.play('C4:3')
```

If you want to change the tempo, set the beats per minutes, as shown in Listing 6-12.

Listing 6-12. Defining Beats per Minutes

```
from microbit import *
import music

music.set_tempo(bpm=180) # set the bpm to 180
music.play('C4:3')
```

You can use the music.set_tempo() function without any parameters to reset the tempo to the default of ticks = 4 and bpm = 120 (see Listing 6-13).

Listing 6-13. Setting the Tempo to the Default Values

```
from microbit import *
import music

music.set_tempo() # set the bpm to 120 and ticks to 4
music.play('C4:3')
```

Getting the Tempo

The music.get_tempo() function returns the current tempo as a tuple of integers. Listing 6-14 shows the MicroPython code that displays the current tempo.

Listing 6-14. Getting the Current Tempo

```
from microbit import *
import music

music.set_tempo(bpm=180, ticks=8) # set the bpm to 180 and
ticks to 8
tempo = music.get_tempo()
print("Current Tempo: ", tempo)
```

First, set the tempo using the music.set_tempo() function with bpm=180 and ticks=8. Then display the current tempo using the music. get_tempo() function. This code will produce the output shown in Figure 6-12.

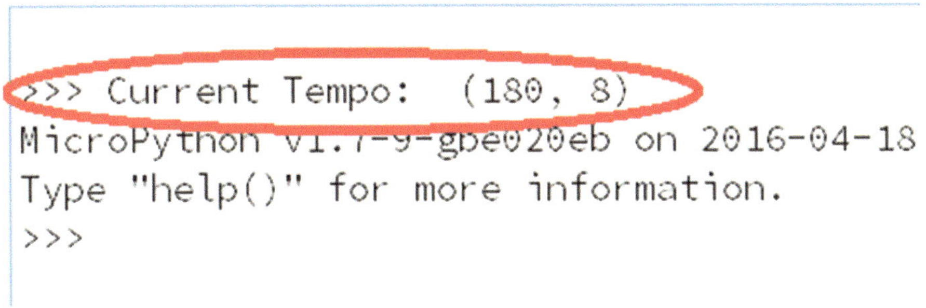

```
>>> Current Tempo:    (180, 8)
MicroPython v1.7-9-gbe020eb on 2016-04-18
Type "help()" for more information.
>>>
```

Figure 6-12. *Displaying the current tempo*

The output shows the current tempo as 180, followed by the number ticks as 8. This function can be used to confirm that you are using the correct tempo in your melody.

Resetting Attributes

Any time you can reset the following musical attributes to the default values with the music.reset() function. They are as follows:

- ticks = 4
- bpm = 120
- duration = 4
- octave = 4

Playing a Pitch

In music, the pitch of a musical note means how high or low the note is. The pitch of a musical note can be measured in a unit called *Hertz*. With MicroPython, you can use the music.pitch() function to set the frequency of a musical note. This function is very similar to the music.play() function that you used. The most important inputs for the music.pitch() function are frequency and duration.

Listing 6-15 shows code that plays a tone at the frequency of 440Hz for one second. The duration is presented in the code as `length` and it should be in milliseconds.

Listing 6-15. Playing a Pitch for a Known Duration

```
from microbit import *
import music

music.pitch(440, 1000)
```

If you want to play a pitch continuously until the blocking call is interrupted, or, in the case of a background call, a new frequency is set or `stop` is called, use a negative number for `len` (i.e., -1). Listing 6-16 shows code that plays a pitch continuously at 440Hz.

Listing 6-16. Playing a Pitch Continuously

```
from microbit import *
import music

music.pitch(440, -1)
```

Summary

In this chapter, you learned how to connect a speaker to the micro:bit in various ways. Then you learned how to code to produce music with micro:bit's built-in melodies and build new melodies with the micro:bit music library. In the next chapter, you learn how use micro:bit's speech API to convert text to speech with punctuation, timbre, and phonemes.

CHAPTER 7

Working with Speech

In the previous chapter, you learned how to use micro:bit's audio capabilities to produce music using the music library. In addition to that, micro:bit provides a speech library to work with text-to-speech conversion that can be used to produce sound similar to the human voice by way of fine tuning various parameters.

Connecting a Speaker

You can use the same wiring diagram that you used in Chapter 6, "Working with Music," to connect a speaker to the micro:bit. Instead of connecting a speaker to the micro:bit pin 0 and GND, you can use the micro:bit's pins 0 and 1 to connect a speaker, as shown in Figure 7-1.

© Pradeeka Seneviratne 2018
P. Seneviratne, *Beginning BBC micro:bit*, https://doi.org/10.1007/978-1-4842-3360-3_7

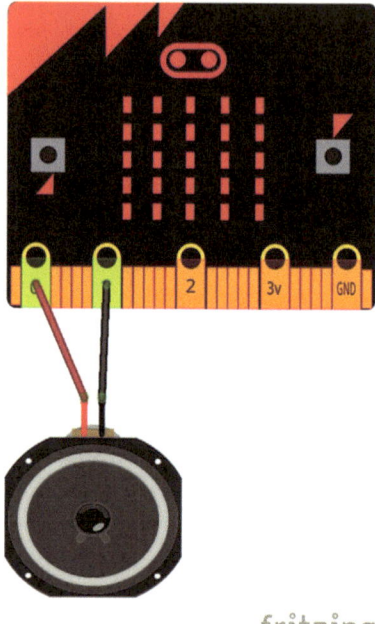

Figure 7-1. *Connecting a speaker to pins 0 and 1*

The speech library provides all the functionalities needed to work with speech and voice related projects. You can import the speech library by adding the import speech statement to the beginning of your program.

Let's start with simple code used to convert text to speech (see Listing 7-1). It converts the text Hello, World to speech and you can hear it from the speaker.

Listing 7-1. Text to Speech Conversion

```
from microbit import *
import speech

speech.say("Hello, World")
```

The `speech.say()` function converts English text to speech and plays it from the attached speaker. When you run this code with micro:bit, you can hear a voice similar to a robot, which is semi-accurate in English. The quality of the voice is not amazing, but it is quite usable. In addition, the `speech.say()` function provides some parameters that you can use to change the default voice.

Timbre

The character or quality of a musical sound or voice is known as its *timbre*. You can change the quality of the default voice by overriding some of the parameters that the speech synthesizer uses to produce it.

Pitch

The pitch defines how high or low the voice sounds. The acceptable values are 0 (high) to 255 (low). You can get a clue about the pitch by hearing the vocals of following singers.

- Highest pitch: Adam Lopez Costa at `https://www.youtube.com/results?search_query=Adam+Lopez+Costa`

- Lowest pitch: Barry White at `https://www.youtube.com/results?search_query=Barry+White`

The default pitch value is 64. Listing 7-2 shows a list of value categories that you can use to set the pitch of the voice.

Listing 7-2. Pitch Categories and Values

```
0-20 impractical
20-30 very high
30-40 high
40-50 high normal
```

```
50-70 normal
70-80 low normal
80-90 low
90-255 very low
```

Listing 7-3 shows the MicroPython code that produces a voice with different pitch categories. The code uses average values in each category.

Listing 7-3. Pitch Levels

```python
from microbit import *
import speech

speech.say("Hello, World")#default pitch is 64
sleep(1000)
speech.say("Hello, World", pitch=10)# impractical
sleep(1000)

speech.say("Hello, World", pitch=25)# very high
sleep(1000)

speech.say("Hello, World", pitch=35)# high
sleep(1000)

speech.say("Hello, World", pitch=45)# high normal
sleep(1000)

speech.say("Hello, World", pitch=60)# normal
sleep(1000)

speech.say("Hello, World", pitch=75)# low normal
sleep(1000)

speech.say("Hello, World", pitch=85)# low
sleep(1000)

speech.say("Hello, World", pitch=170)# very low
```

Speed

Speed defines how quickly the device talks. The acceptable values are from 0 (impossible) to 255 (like bedtime story). The default value is 72. Listing 7-4 shows a list of categories and values to define the speed.

Listing 7-4. Speed Categories and Values

```
0-20 impractical
20-40 very fast
40-60 fast
60-70 fast conversational
70-75 normal conversational
75-90 narrative
90-100 slow
100-225 very slow
```

Listing 7-5 shows the code that speaks the text Hello, World in different speeds.

Listing 7-5. Speak with Different Speeds

```python
from microbit import *
import speech

speech.say("Hello, World")#default speed is 72
sleep(1000)
speech.say("Hello, World", speed=10) # impractical
sleep(1000)
speech.say("Hello, World", speed=30) # very fast
sleep(1000)
speech.say("Hello, World", speed=50) # fast
sleep(1000)
speech.say("Hello, World", speed=65) # fast conversational
sleep(1000)
```

```
speech.say("Hello, World", speed=73) # normal conversational
sleep(1000)
speech.say("Hello, World", speed=83) # narrative
sleep(1000)
speech.say("Hello, World", speed=95) # slow
sleep(1000)
speech.say("Hello, World", speed=175) # very slow
sleep(1000)
```

Mouth

Mouth defines how tight-lipped or overtly enunciating the voice sounds (0 = tight-lipped, 255 = Foghorn Leghorn).

- Tight-lipped: The most extreme example of this is a ventriloquist, which is a person who changes his or her voice so that it appears that the voice is coming from elsewhere.

- Overtly enunciating: A good example of this is Foghorn Leghorn, who was a cartoon character that has appeared in the Looney Tunes and Merrie Melodies cartoons of Warner Bros. (See https://www.youtube.com/results?search_query=Foghorn+Leghorn.)

Listing 7-6 shows some sample code with the mouth parameter.

Listing 7-6. Controlling the Mouth Parameter

```
from microbit import *
import speech

speech.say("Hello, World", mouth=200)
```

Throat

Throat defines how relaxed or tense the tone of voice is (0 = falling apart, 255 = totally chilled).

Listing 7-7 shows some sample code with the throat parameter.

Listing 7-7. Controlling the Throat Parameter

```
from microbit import *
import speech

speech.say("Hello, World", throat=100)
```

Example: Creating a Robotic Voice

The default voice produced by a speech synthesizer can be tuned with the parameters just discussed (pitch, speed, mouth, and throat) to produce a robotic voice.

Listing 7-8 shows some sample code that can be used to produce a voice similar to a robot. The speech.say() function combines all the given parameters to produce the voice for the given text.

Listing 7-8. Voice of a Robot

```
from microbit import *
import speech

speech.say("I am a baker bot", speed=120, pitch=100,
throat=100, mouth=200)
```

Punctuation

Punctuation makes a voice more realistic. With a speech library, you can use five types of punctuation to alter the delivery of speech. They are as follows:

- *Hyphen*: Creates a short pause in the speech.

  ```
  speech.say("I am a baker bot - crazy cooking",
  speed=120, pitch=100, throat=100, mouth=200)
  ```

- *Comma:* Adds a pause of approximately double that of the hyphen.

  ```
  speech.say("I am a baker bot, crazy cooking",
  speed=120, pitch=100, throat=100, mouth=200)
  ```

- *Full stop:* Creates a pause and causes the pitch to fall.

  ```
  speech.say("I am a baker bot - crazy cooking.",
  speed=120, pitch=100, throat=100, mouth=200)
  ```

- *Question mark:* Creates a pause and causes the pitch to rise.

  ```
  speech.say("I am a baker bot. Who are you?", speed=120,
  pitch=100, throat=100, mouth=200)
  ```

Phonemes

Phonemes can be used to translate English words into the correct sounds. They are the building blocks of language. The `speech.pronounce()` function allows you to translate any phoneme into the correct voice in English.

An example, the word Hello can be written with phonemes as /HEHLOW. Listing 7-9 shows the MicroPython code used to produce the voice using phonemes.

Listing 7-9. Phonemes

```
from microbit import *
import speech

speech.pronounce("/HEHLOW")  # "Hello"
```

You can convert any English text to a string of phonemes using the speech.translate() function (see Listing 7-10). Then you can fine tune the phonemes to produce a more natural voice.

Listing 7-10. Translate the Text to Phonemes

```
from microbit import *
import speech

print(speech.translate("Hello"))
```

The following table lists the phonemes understood by the synthesizer (Source: http://microbit-micropython.readthedocs.io/en/latest/speech.html).

SIMPLE VOWELS		VOICED CONSONANTS	
IY	f(ee)t	R	(r)ed
IH	p(i)n	L	a(ll)ow
EH	b(e)g	W	a(w)ay
AE	S(a)m	W	(wh)ale
AA	p(o)t	Y	(y)ou
AH	b(u)dget	M	(S)am
AO	t(al)k	N	ma(n)
OH	c(o)ne	NX	so(ng)
UH	b(oo)k	B	(b)ad
UX	l(oo)t	D	(d)og
ER	b(ir)d	G	a(g)ain
AX	gall(o)n	J	(j)u(dg)e
IX	dig(i)t	Z	(z)oo
		ZH	plea(s)ure
DIPHTHONGS		V	se(v)en
EY	m(a)de	DH	(th)en
AY	h(igh)		
OY	b(oy)		
AW	h(ow)	UNVOICED CONSONANTS	
OW	sl(ow)	S	(S)am
UW	cr(ew)	SH	fi(sh)
		F	(f)ish
		TH	(th)in
SPECIAL PHONEMES		P	(p)oke
UL	sett(le) (=AXL)	T	(t)alk
UM	astron(om)y (=AXM)	K	(c)ake
UN	functi(on) (=AXN)	CH	spee(ch)
Q	kitt-en (glottal stop)	/H	a(h)ead

Here is a list of non-standard symbols:

YX	diphthong ending (weaker version of Y)
WX	diphthong ending (weaker version of W)
RX	R after a vowel (smooth version of R)
LX	L after a vowel (smooth version of L)
/X	H before a non-front vowel **or** consonant - **as in** (wh)o
DX	T **as in** pi(t)y (weaker version of T)

Here is a list of some seldom used phoneme combinations:

```
PHONEME       YOU PROBABLY WANT:    UNLESS IT SPLITS SYLLABLES LIKE:
COMBINATION
GS            GZ e.g. ba(gs)        bu(gs)pray
BS            BZ e.g. slo(bz)       o(bsc)ene
DS            DZ e.g. su(ds)        Hu(ds)son
PZ            PS e.g. sla(ps)       -----
TZ            TS e.g. cur(ts)y      -----
KZ            KS e.g. fi(x)         -----
NG            NXG e.g. singing      i(ng)rate
NK            NXK e.g. bank         Su(nk)ist
```

Using lmtool

lmtool (see `http://www.speech.cs.cmu.edu/tools/lmtool-new.html`) provides an easy way to convert English text to phonemes. Use the following steps to convert a text file to a Pronunciation Dictionary file using lmtool.

1. Using a text editor, create a file with your sentence (or many sentences) in English. You should include at least two words in your file, otherwise the compilation will fail. Then, save the file on your computer (see Figure 7-2).

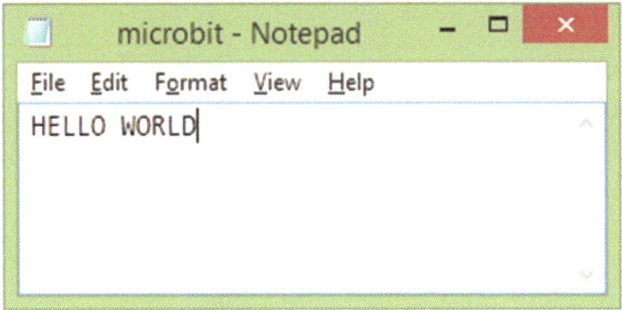

Figure 7-2. *Source file with text*

2. Browse and locate the saved file by clicking the Choose File button (see Figure 7-3).

3. Click the Compile Knowledge Base button (see Figure 7-3).

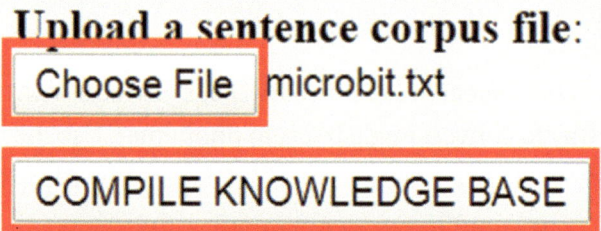

To use: Create a sentence corpus file, cc a line (but do not need to have standard fragments to recombine into new senten

Upload a sentence corpus file:
Choose File   microbit.txt

COMPILE KNOWLEDGE BASE

Figure 7-3. *Uploading and compiling a text file*

4. On the results page, click the file name with the .dic extension (see Figure 7-4). This is the Pronunciation Dictionary file.

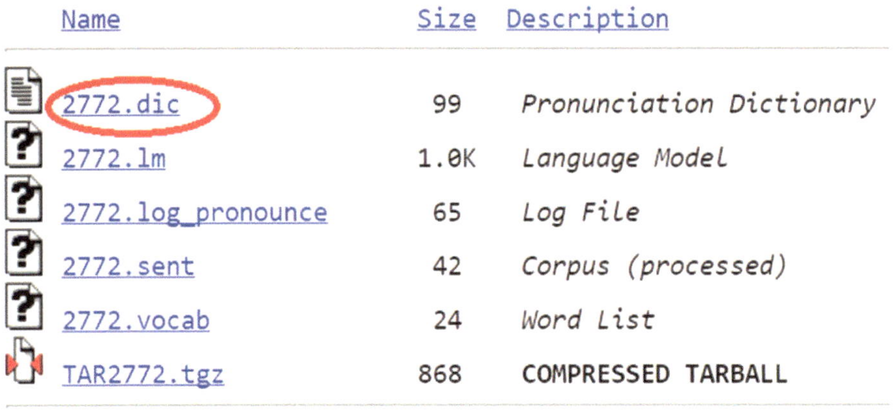

Name	Size	Description
2772.dic	99	*Pronunciation Dictionary*
2772.lm	1.0K	*Language Model*
2772.log_pronounce	65	*Log File*
2772.sent	42	*Corpus (processed)*
2772.vocab	24	*Word List*
TAR2772.tgz	868	**COMPRESSED TARBALL**

Figure 7-4. *Pronunciation Dictionary file*

5. The file contains phonemes for each word in the
    sentence (see Figure 7-5). As you can see, the tool
    suggests two phonemes for the word "Hello". Choose
    the most relevant phoneme for your micro:bit
    application.

```
HELLO    HH AH L OW
HELLO(2)         HH EH L OW
WORLD    W ER L D
```

Figure 7-5. *Phonemes for each word*

Stress Markers

Stress markers can be used to create a more expressive tone of voice.
They range from 1-8. You can insert the required number after the vowel
to create stress. For example, the lack of expression of /HEHLOW can be
improved by inserting stress marker 3 followed by the vowel EH, as in
/HEH3LOW. Listing 7-11 shows a list of stress markers.

Listing 7-11. Stress Markers

```
1- very emotional stress
2- very emphatic stress
3- rather strong stress
4- ordinary stress
5- tight stress
6- neutral (no pitch change) stress
7 - pitch-dropping stress
8- extreme pitch-dropping stress
```

Listing 7-12 shows the MicroPython code that produces a much improved voice for the word "Hello" by inserting a stress marker.

Listing 7-12. Stress Markers

```
from microbit import *
import speech

speech.pronounce("/HEH3LOW")  # "Hello"
```

Singing with Phonemes

The speech.sing() function can be used to sign phonemes. Listing 7-13 shows the lyrics for a happy birthday song.

Listing 7-13. Lyrics for the Happy Birthday Song

```
Happy Birthday to You
Happy Birthday to You
Happy Birthday Dear Micro Bit
Happy Birthday to You
```

First, you need to convert the text to phonemes, as shown in Listing 7-14. You can use the speech.translate() function or lmtool to convert the text into phonemes.

Listing 7-14. Phonemes for the Happy Birthday Song

```
HH AE P IY B ER TH D EY T UW Y UW
HH AE P IY B ER TH D EY T UW Y UW
HH AE P IY B ER TH D EY D IH R M AY K R OW B IH T
HH AE P IY B ER TH D EY T UW Y UW
```

Listing 7-15 shows the MicroPython code used to sing a happy birthday song with phonemes.

Listing 7-15. Sing a Song with Phonemes

```
from microbit import *
import speech

speech.sing("#115 /H AE P IY B ER TH D EY T UW Y UW",
speed=100)
speech.sing("#115 /H AE P IY B ER TH D EY T UW Y UW",
speed=100)
speech.sing("#115 /H AE P IY B ER TH D EY D IH R M AY K R OW B
IH T", speed=100) speech.sing("#115 /H AE P IY B ER TH D EY T
UW Y UW", speed=100)
```

You can change the value of the speed parameter to control the speed of the song. The pitch number 115 is used with a hash (#115) as an annotation. You can also add other parameters—such as pitch, mouth, and throat—to change the timbre (quality) of the voice.

Summary

In this chapter, you learned how to produce voices and songs using the micro:bit speech library. You learned how to emulate different voices by changing the characteristics of the voice.

The next chapter explains how to store and manipulate files with micro:bit's internal storage.

CHAPTER 8

Storing and Manipulating Files

micro:bit provides a persistent file system that allows you to store files in the flash memory. The size of the storage reserved for the file system is approximately 30KB. However, micro:bit provides a flat file system, so you can't store files in directories to create a hierarchy. The stored files will remain intact until you either delete them or re-flash the device.

In this chapter, you learn how to store files in the micro:bit internal storage and manipulate them with some OS functions. Then you learn about the MicroFS utility that can be used to manipulate files on micro:bit and transfer files between micro:bit and the computer.

Creating a File

With micro:bit, you can create files with any extension. The open() function allows you to create a file for a given name with the w parameter for writing. This function will also overwrite the contents of the file if it exists. The write() function can be used to write a line of text into the file.

© Pradeeka Seneviratne 2018
P. Seneviratne, *Beginning BBC micro:bit*, https://doi.org/10.1007/978-1-4842-3360-3_8

Flash the sample code in Listing 8-1 to your micro:bit using the Mu editor. After the flashing is done, click on the Files button. The Mu editor will display all the files in your micro:bit storage under the Files on Your micro:bit list view (see Figure 8-1) . You can see that the file named foo. txt has been created on your micro:bit with the given content, which is a single line of text.

Listing 8-1. Creating a File

```
with open('foo.txt', 'w') as myFile:
    myFile.write("This is the first line")
```

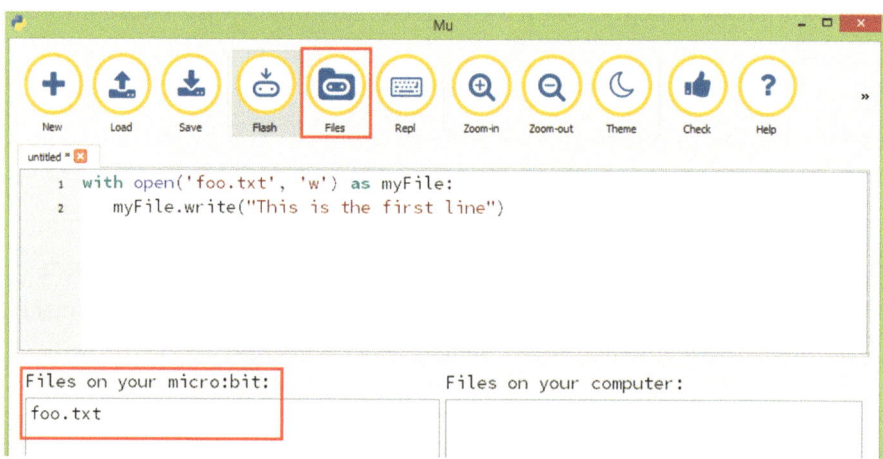

Figure 8-1. *Files window*

Reading a File

You can also read a file with the open() function. You must provide the file name with the extension and the optional argument r to open the file for reading in text mode.

You can read the contents of the foo.txt file, as shown here.

1. Click again on the Files button to close the Files window.

2. Click the Repl button to start a new REPL session (an interactive shell).

3. Run the code shown in Listing 8-2 using the Repl window. Press the Enter key followed by each line.

Note   Don't flash the code shown in Listing 8-2 to the micro:bit. Flashing a new code to the micro:bit will destroy all the stored files in the micro:bit internal storage.

Listing 8-2. Reading a File

```
with open('foo.txt') as myFile:
   print(myFile.read())
```

4. When you press the Enter key followed by the last line, you will get the contents of the file as the output (see Figure 8-2).

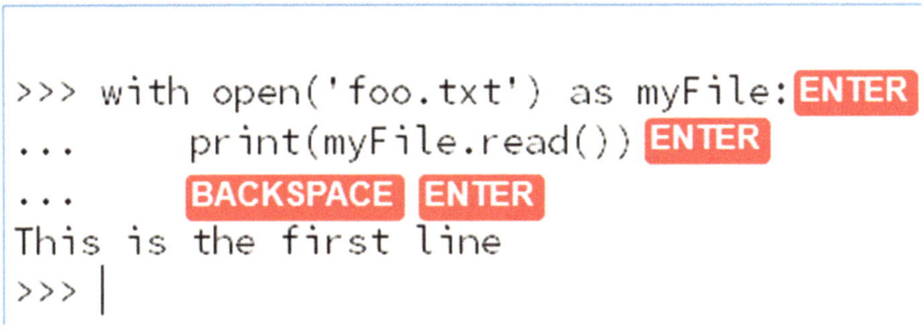

Figure 8-2. Reading the contents of a file

Writing Multiple Lines in a File

When you are creating or overwriting a file, you can write multiple lines in a file. The `write()` function can be called any number of times with your code for each line of text. Listing 8-3 shows the sample code that uses the `write()` function for each line of text. However, remember to add a new line character \n at the end of each line before starting a new line.

Flash the sample code to the micro:bit using the Mu editor. This will create the file called `foo.txt` on the micro:bit internal storage with the given content.

Listing 8-3. Creating a File with Multiple Lines of Text

```
with open('foo.txt', 'w') as myFile:
    myFile.write("This is the first line\n")
    myFile.write("This is the second line")
```

You can also write the two lines of text using a single `write()` function as shown here.

```
myFile.write("This is the first line\nThis is the second line")
```

After flashing the code, you can read the contents of the `foo.txt` file with the `read()` command. Start a new REPL session by clicking on the Repl button and entering the code into the REPL window, as shown in Figure 8-3. After executing the complete code, you will get the contents of the file as the output on the REPL window.

```
>>> with open('foo.txt') as myFile: ENTER
...        print(myFile.read()) ENTER
...        BACKSPACE ENTER
This is the first line
This is the second line
>>>
```

Figure 8-3. *Reading the contents of a file*

Appending Text to a File

micro:bit doesn't provide a function to append text to a file after creating it. However, there is a way you can append text to an existing file using a tricky mechanism. The implementation of the append operation is explained here.

1. Read the contents of the existing file and store it in a variable.

2. Add new text to the stored content.

3. Create the file again with the same name (this will overwrite the existing file) and write the stored contents to the file at the same time.

Assume you created a file named foo.txt with a single line of text. Now you are going to add another line of text to the file. Figure 8-4 shows how to do this with a REPL session (*don't flash it to the micro:bit!*). It also shows the final contents of the foo.txt file after appending the second line of text.

```
>>> with open('foo.txt') as myFile1: ENTER
...      content = myFile1.read() ENTER
...      content = content + '\nThis is the second line' ENTER
...      print(content) ENTER
... BACKSPACE ENTER
This is the first line
This is the second line
>>> with open('foo.txt', 'w') as myFile2: ENTER
...      myFile2.write(content) ENTER
... BACKSPACE ENTER
...
46
>>> with open('foo.txt') as myFile3: ENTER
...      print(myFile3.read()) ENTER
... BACKSPACE ENTER
This is the first line
This is the second line
>>>
```

Figure 8-4. *Appending text to a file*

Creating Files with a .py Extension

If a file ends with the .py extension, it can be imported to your code. For example, a file named hello.py can be imported like so:

```
import hello.
```

This will output any statement written with the print function in the Python file.

Create the foo.py file as shown in Listing 8-4 using the Mu editor and then flash it to the micro:bit.

Listing 8-4. Creating the foo.py File

```
with open('foo.py', 'w') as myFile:
    myFile.write("i=10\n")
    myFile.write("print('-------------')\n")
    myFile.write("print(i)\n")
    myFile.write("print('-------------')")
```

176

After flashing the file, start a new REPL session and type this statement:

```
import foo
```

When you press the Enter key followed by this statement, you will get the output shown in Figure 8-5. This indicates that when you run the `import` command followed by the file name, the file gets executed (not the contents of the file) and the result will print to the console.

```
>>> import foo ENTER
------------------
10
------------------
>>>
```

Figure 8-5. Output for foo.py with a REPL session

However, you can print the contents of this file using the `read()` function. Figure 8-6 shows the complete REPL session to get the contents of the `foo.py` file with the `read()` function.

```
>>> with open('foo.py') as myFile: ENTER
...        print(myFile.read()) ENTER
... BACKSPACE ENTER
i=10
print('-------------')
print(i)
print('-------------')
>>>
```

Figure 8-6. Using the read() function to get the contents of the foo.py file

Creating Your Own Libraries

You can now import any valid Python file to your code. A Python file that contains a function or set of functions is called a *library*. In this section, you'll see how to use a function in an external Python file with your code. First create a Python file named `gereeting.py` with a simple function. Listing 8-5 shows the MicroPython code that can be used to create the `greeting.py` file with a simple function named `showGreeting()`.

Listing 8-5. Creating a Python Library

```
with open('greeting.py', 'w') as myFile:
    myFile.write("def showGreeting():\n")
    myFile.write("  print('Hello Friend!')")
```

You can use this Python library using a REPL session with Mu, as shown in Figure 8-7. First you must import the Python file stored in the internal storage with this command:

```
import greeting
```

Then you can call the function as follows:

```
greeting.showGreeting()
```

Figure 8-7. *Using a Python library*

File Manipulation

micro:bit allows you to manipulate the files stored in internal storage. The os library provides some useful functions to work with the micro:bit file system.

Before working with the examples given in file manipulation, first create some files in the microbit internal storage using the code shown in Listing 8-6.

Listing 8-6. Creating Four Files on micro:bit Storage

```
with open('foo.txt', 'w') as foo:
    foo.write("foo")
with open('bar.txt', 'w') as bar:
    bar.write("bar")
with open('baz.py', 'w') as baz:
    baz.write("a=5")
with open('qux.py', 'w') as qux:
    qux.write("b=7")
```

Listing Files

You can list all the files stored in your micro:bit using the `listdir()` function. First, open a REPL session and run these statements.

```
import os
os.listdir()
```

The `litsdir()` function will return the list of files stored in your micro:bit storage. Figure 8-8 shows the complete REPL session with the output.

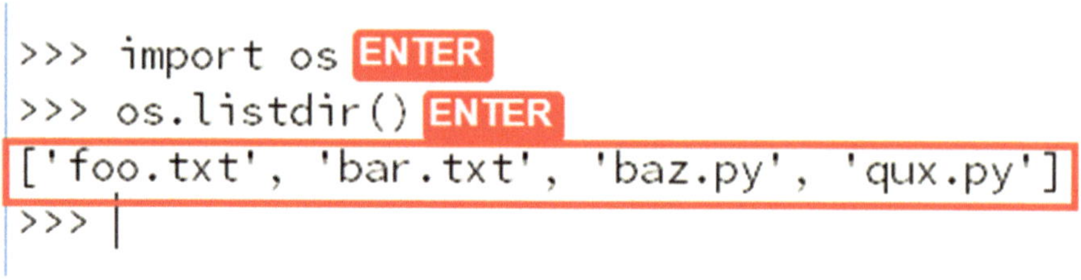

```
>>> import os ENTER
>>> os.listdir() ENTER
['foo.txt', 'bar.txt', 'baz.py', 'qux.py']
>>>
```

Figure 8-8. *Listing files on micro:bit storage*

Deleting Files

You can delete a file using the remove() function. Now you're going to delete the foo.txt file stored on the micro:bit storage.

Using the same REPL session, run the following statement:

os.remove('foo.txt')

After running the remove() function to delete the file, run the listdir() function again to verify that the file is deleted. Figure 8-9 shows the REPL session with output.

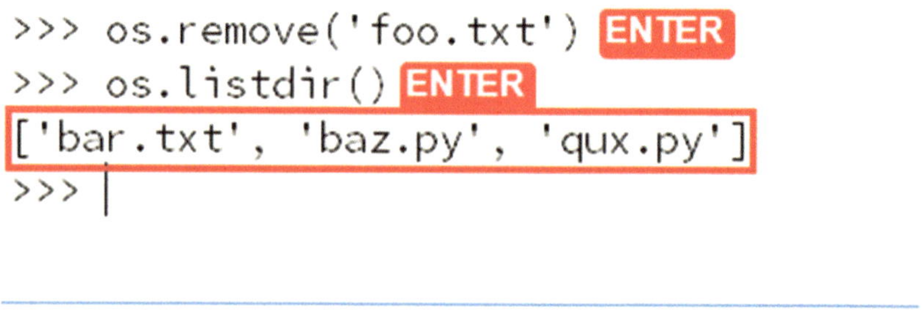

```
>>> os.remove('foo.txt') ENTER
>>> os.listdir() ENTER
['bar.txt', 'baz.py', 'qux.py']
>>>
```

Figure 8-9. *REPL session for deleting a file*

Getting the Size of a File

The size() function can be used to get the size of a file stored on the micro:bit storage. It returns the size of a given file in bytes. Let's get the size of the file named bar.txt by running the following statement with the same REPL session.

```
print(os.size('bar.txt'))
```

The size() function returns the size of the bar.txt file, which is three bytes.

Figure 8-10 shows the REPL session with the output.

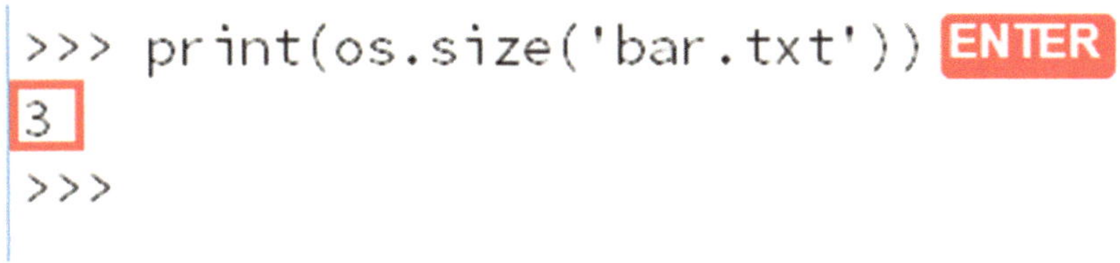

```
>>> print(os.size('bar.txt')) ENTER
3
>>>
```

Figure 8-10. *Getting the size of a file*

File Transfer with MicroFS

MicroFS is a simple command-line tool that can be used to interact with the limited file system provided by MicroPython on the micro:bit.

Installing MicroFS

You can install MicroFS on a computer running Windows, Linux, or Mac operating systems. The details in this section can be directly applied to installing MicroFS on all three of these operating systems.

Before installing MicroFS, determine whether you already have Python and `pip` installed on your computer as prerequisites. If you don't have Python and `pip`, install them on your computer using these sources:

- **Python**: `https://www.python.org/downloads/`

- **pip**: `https://pip.pypa.io//en/latest/installing/`

From now on, the Windows command prompt is used to demonstrate the installation and use of MicroFS.

After setting up everything, simply run the following command from the Windows command prompt (see Figure 8-11):

```
$ pip install microfs
```

This will install MicroFS on your Windows computer in a few minutes.

```
E:\>pip install microfs
Collecting microfs
  Downloading microfs-1.2.1.tar.gz
Collecting pyserial (from microfs)
  Downloading pyserial-3.4-py2.py3-none-any.whl (193kB)
    100% |████████████████████████████████| 194kB 481kB/s
Building wheels for collected packages: microfs
  Running setup.py bdist_wheel for microfs ... done
  Stored in directory: C:\Users\Pasindu\AppData\Local\pip\Cache\wheels\94\c4\10\
9ac4b445f4436b4b15a3b2e1c5091908a576e48fb31c2004bc
Successfully built microfs
Installing collected packages: pyserial, microfs
Successfully installed microfs-1.2.1 pyserial-3.4

E:\>
```

Figure 8-11. *Installing MicroFS*

Upgrading MicroFS

After installing MicroFS, you can upgrade it by using this command (see Figure 8-12):

```
pip install –no-cache –upgrade microfs
```

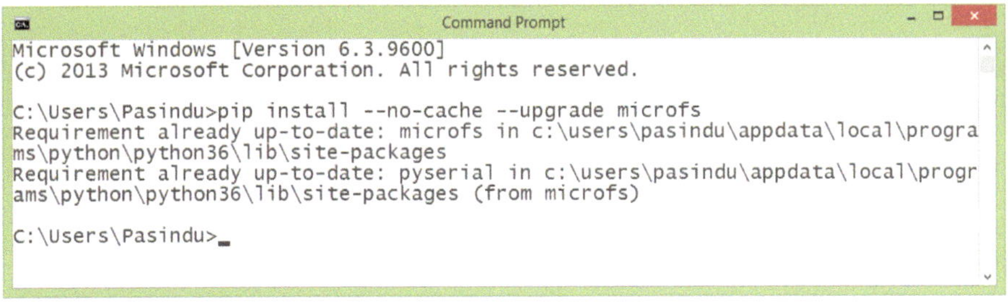

```
Command Prompt                                    _ □ ×
Microsoft Windows [Version 6.3.9600]
(c) 2013 Microsoft Corporation. All rights reserved.

C:\Users\Pasindu>pip install --no-cache --upgrade microfs
Requirement already up-to-date: microfs in c:\users\pasindu\appdata\local\progra
ms\python\python36\lib\site-packages
Requirement already up-to-date: pyserial in c:\users\pasindu\appdata\local\progr
ams\python\python36\lib\site-packages (from microfs)

C:\Users\Pasindu>_
```

Figure 8-12. *Upgrading MicroFS*

Now you are ready to access your micro:bit using the MicroFS utility. You should start every command with ufs:

$ufs [command]

List the Files on the micro:bit

The ls command can list all the files in your micro:bit storage:

$ufs ls

Assume there are three files created on your micro:bit storage (see Figure 8-13). If you want to run the commands in this section with the same examples, first create three files named bar.txt, baz.py, and qux.py on your micro:bit.

183

```
Files on your micro:bit:
bar.txt
baz.py
qux.py
```

Figure 8-13. *Three files created on the micro:bit*

Figure 8-14 shows you how to run the `ls` command from the command prompt. After running the `ls` command, you should get the names of three files as the result.

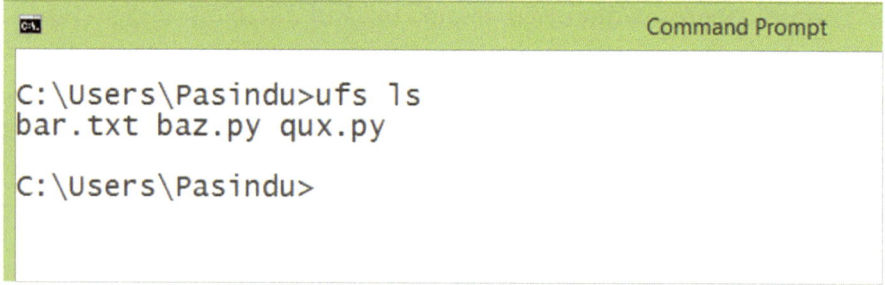

Figure 8-14. *Listing all the files on micro:bit*

Copy a File from the micro:bit

The get command can be used to transfer any file from the micro:bit to your computer:

```
$ufs get bar.txt
```

After running the get command, the targeted file will be saved on the local drive of your computer. (You can find the copied file on your computer's hard drive by following the current directory of the command prompt.)

Figure 8-15 shows how to run the get command from the command prompt. After running the command, the dir command can be run from the command prompt to verify whether the file is copied to the computer.

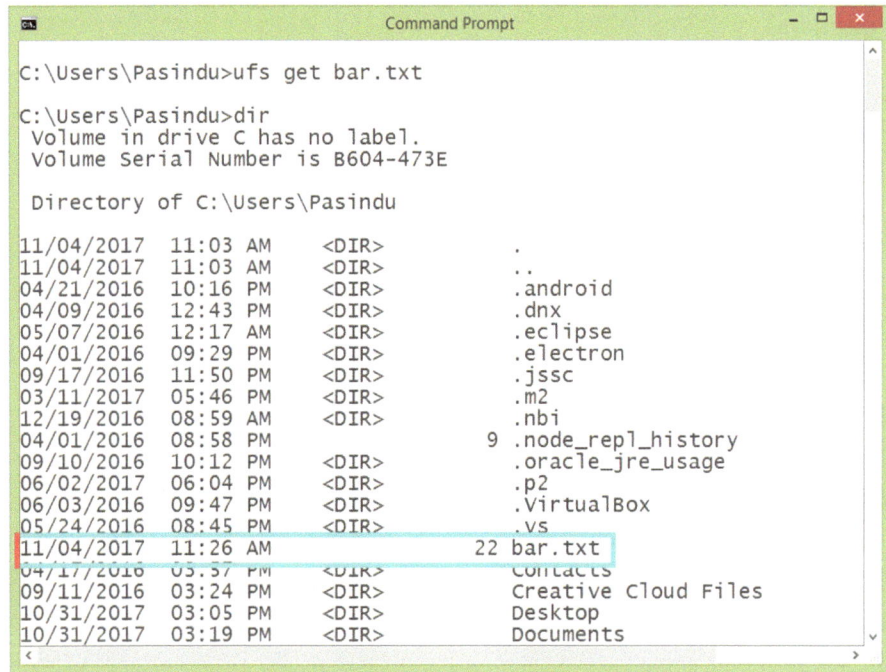

Figure 8-15. *Copying a file from micro:bit followed by verifying it*

Copy a File to the micro:bit

You can copy any file from your computer to micro:bit using the put command:

```
$ ufs put path/to/file.txt
```

As an example, if you want to copy the file named led.py on your computer to micro:bit, run the command shown here. This example assumes that the file is currently located in the D:/microbit/files/ directory.

```
$ufs put d:/microbit/files/led.py
```

Figure 8-16 shows how to run the put command from the command prompt. After running the put command, you can verify it using the ls command.

Figure 8-16. *Copying a file to the micro:bit followed by verifying it*

Deleting a File on the micro:bit

The rm command can be used to delete a file on the micro:bit. An example, if you want to delete the qux.py file on your micro:bit, issue this command.

```
$ ufs rm qux.py
```

Figure 8-17 shows you how to run the rm command from the command prompt. After running the rm command, you can verify it using the ls command.

```
C:\Users\Pasindu>ufs rm qux.py

C:\Users\Pasindu>ufs ls
bar.txt baz.py led.py

C:\Users\Pasindu>_
```

Figure 8-17. *Deleting a file on the micro:bit followed by verifying it*

Summary

In this chapter, you learned how to use the micro:bit's file system to store and manipulate files with the os module. You also learned how to use the MicroFS utility to manipulate files on micro:bit as well as how to transfer files between micro:bit and your computer.

In next chapter, you learn how to build applications based on micro:bit wired and wireless (radio) networks.

CHAPTER 9

Networks and Radios

Networking micro:bits together allows you to exchange data and broadcast to many micro:bit boards. In this chapter, you learn how to build wired and wireless networks with micro:bit boards. You'll be able to build a wide range of applications based on the networking features of the micro:bit, such as data loggers, remote control vehicles, advertising beacons, and many more.

Building a Wired Network

Wired networks allow you to connect two or more micro:bit boards using wires. However, this architecture doesn't support any addressing and grouping features. Therefore, this type of network is more suitable to connect two micro:bit boards.

You need the following things to build a simple wired network.

- Two crocodile leads
- Two micro:bit boards
- Two battery cases
- Four AA batteries

Connect the two micro:bit boards using the crocodile leads, as shown in Figure 9-1.

© Pradeeka Seneviratne 2018

P. Seneviratne, *Beginning BBC micro:bit*, https://doi.org/10.1007/978-1-4842-3360-3_9

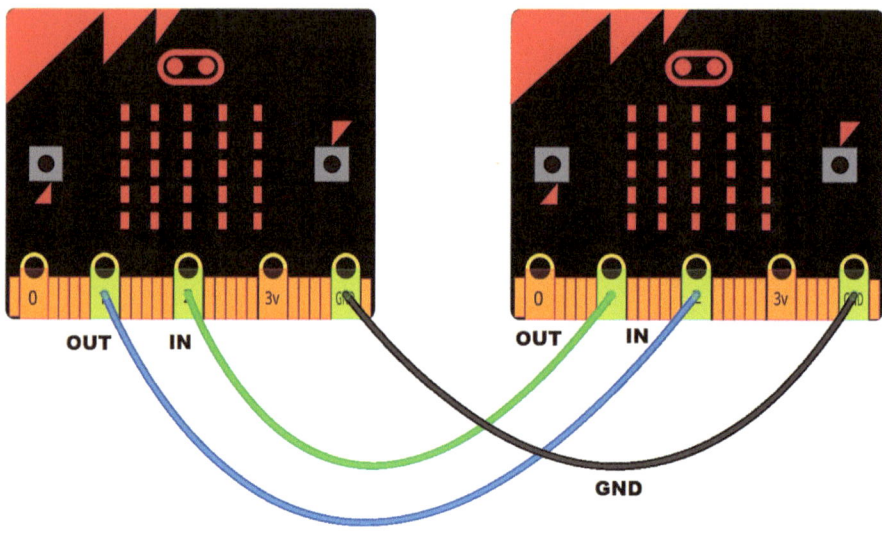

Figure 9-1. *Connecting two micro:bit boards for networking*

Before make the connections, you must decide which pins you are going to use for input and output on both micro:bit boards.

This example uses pin 2 for input and pin 1 for output. This will apply to both boards, so both boards know what to do with each pin.

Here are the two MicroPython statements that you can use to write digital 1 and 0 on pin 1 (OUT):

```
pin1.write_digital(1)  # switch the signal on
pin1.write_digital(0)  # switch the signal off
```

You can also read the incoming signal on pin 2 (IN) with this MicroPython statement:

```
input = pin2.read_digital()  # read the value of the signal
(either 1 or 0)
```

Let's build a basic application based on the micro:bit wired network. Assume that you have two micro:bit boards labeled X and Y, wired as discussed previously.

When you press and hold built-in button A on the micro:bit board X, an image should display on the micro:bit board Y. Similarly, when you press and hold built-in button A on the micro:bit board Y, an image should display on the micro:bit board X. The implementation is very simple, as shown in Listing 9-1 with MicroPython code.

Listing 9-1. Basic micro:bit Network Application

```
from microbit import *

while True:
    if button_a.is_pressed():
        pin1.write_digital(1)
    else:
        pin1.write_digital(0)

    input = pin2.read_digital()
    if (input == 1):
        display.show(Image.HAPPY)
    else:
        display.clear()
```

Flash the code into both micro:bit boards. According to the code, when you press and release button A, it will write digital 1 on pin 1; otherwise, the value on pin 1 is 0 (OUT). Meanwhile, it will read the incoming values (IN) on pin 2. If it finds that the incoming value is 1, it will display an image on the LED display.

Buffering Incoming Data

Buffering is useful for storing data temporarily for processing when required. Listing 9-2 shows how to send data and buffer receiving data with MicroPython using the same hardware setup shown in Figure 9-1.

According to the code, when you press and release built-in button A, the value on pin 1 becomes 1 (HIGH).

When receiving, micro:bit stores all the digital 1 (HIGH) status on pin 2 in the variable named buffer. It ignores digital 0 (LOW) status. At any time, you can press built-in button B to see all the buffered 1 (HIGH) status on the LED display.

Flash the code into both micro:bit boards. Label these two boards as X and Y. Now test the code.

1. Press and release button A five times on micro:bit board X.

2. Then press and release built-in button B on the micro:bit board Y to see the output on the LED display. Five x marks will scroll on the LED display to indicate the five button pressed events. See Listing 9-2.

Listing 9-2. Buffering Data

```
from microbit import *

buffer = ''
while True:
    # Sending
    if button_a.was_pressed():
        pin1.write_digital(1)
    else:
        pin1.write_digital(0)
```

```
# Receiving
if (pin2.read_digital() == 1):
    buffer += 'x '

if button_b.was_pressed():
    display.scroll(buffer)
    buffer = ''
sleep(100)
```

Using Radios

Micro:bit's CPU (central processing unit) has a built-in 2.4GHz radio module that allows you to send and receive messages wirelessly with the radio library. With the radio library, you can build a wide range of applications that can be used to exchange data between micro:bit boards.

Turning the Radio On and Off

The radio.on() function allows you to turn on the radio module and send and receive messages. You can turn off the radio by simply calling the radio.off() function. Listing 9-3 shows the MicroPython code needed to turn on the micro:bit radio for five seconds.

Listing 9-3. Turn On the micro:bit Radio for Five Seconds

```
from microbit import *
import radio
radio.on() # turns the radio on
sleep(5000)
radio.off() # turns the radio off
```

Sending and Receiving Messages

You can send messages up to 251 bytes long (or 250 characters per message) with the radio.send() function.

Sending messages are similar to broadcasting programs from a radio station. All radios can receive the same program if they are tuned to the correct frequency. Similarly, micro:bit boards will receive the message within the transmission range if they are configured to receive.

This can be demonstrated by using two micro:bit boards. Listing 9-4 shows the MicroPython code to send a message to the other micro:bit board. The code should be saved onto the first micro:bit board.

Listing 9-4. Sending a Message

```
from microbit import *
import radio

while True:
    radio.on() # turns the radio on
    message = "Hello,World!."
    radio.send(message)
sleep(500)
```

Micro:bits may receive a message using the radio.receive() function. Listing 9-5 shows the MicroPython code that should be saved onto the second micro:bit board so the message can be received and displayed.

Listing 9-5. Receiving Incoming Messages

```
from microbit import *
import radio

radio.on()

while True:
```

```
incoming = radio.receive()
if incoming is not None:
    display.show(incoming)
    # print(incoming)
sleep(500)
```

Configuring Radio

By now, you know how to send and receive messages using the micro:bit radio module. All of the previous examples used the micro:bit radio's default configuration settings to send and receive messages. If you use the default configuration settings, you can send the same message to every micro:bit board that has the default configuration. You can configure the radio module using the `radio.config()` function.

Selecting a Channel

Like a radio or TV transmitter, the micro:bit radio module can be configured with a transmission frequency. The same frequency will receive the data too. The `channel` keyword can be used to set the channel number, as shown here.

```
radio.config(channel=25)
```

The micro:bit supports a total of 101 channels for general use, numbered 0 to 100, with the default channel set to 7.

Channel 0 has a frequency of 2400Mhz and each channel has a bandwidth of 1Mhz. For example, channel 1 will be at 2401Mhz, channel 2 at 2402MhZ, and so forth.

Defining Groups

You can assign your micro:bit to a virtual group using the group keyword. Groups allow you to create more than one micro:bit radio project in the same network range without interfering with messages. Remember, your micro:bit can only ever be a member of one group at a time, and any packets sent will only be received by other micro:bits in the same group. You can use a group number from 0 to 255. The default group number is 0.

```
radio.config(group=7)
```

Assigning Addresses

Assigning an address to the micro:bit radio module allows you to filter the incoming messages at the hardware level, keeping only those that match the address you set. You can express an address as a 32-bit address. The default address used is 0x75626974. The address keyword can be used to set the address for the radio.

```
radio.config(address=0x11111111)
```

Transmission Power

Transmission power of the radio module indicates the strength of the signal and how far it can go from the source. You can set the transmission power for the micro:bit radio module using the radio.power() function. This function accepts values from 0 to 7; the default is 6. The higher the value, the more power the radio module consumes from the micro:bit. However, using a strong signal will help you reach more micro:bit radio modules.

```
radio.config (power = 7)
```

Remotely Controlling an LED

You can build a wide range of wireless applications using the micro:bit radio module. As a first example, let's write MicroPython code to control an LED remotely.

Figure 9-2 shows the wiring diagram for connecting an LED with the micro:bit. Connect the positive leg (anode) of the LED with micro:bit pin 0 and the negative leg (cathode) of the LED with the micro:bit GND through a 220 Ohm resistor.

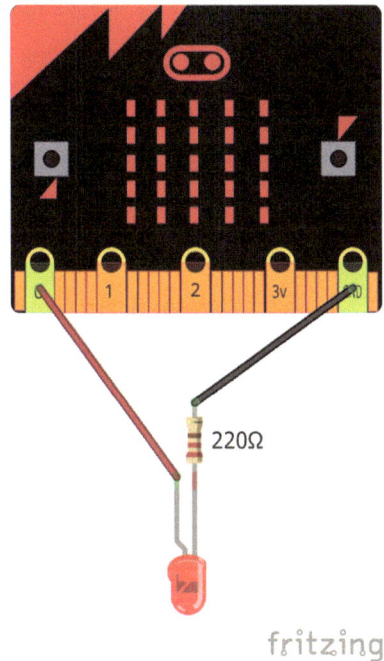

Figure 9-2. *Wiring diagram for connecting an LED with micro:bit*

Listing 9-6 shows the MicroPython code you can flash to the micro:bit board that you are going to use as the remote control (the sender).

197

Listing 9-6. Remote Control (Sender)

```
from microbit import *
import radio

radio.on() # turns the radio on
radio.config(power=7)

while True:
    if(button_a.was_pressed()): # to turn the remote LED on
        radio.send("H") # sends letter H to receiver
    elif(button_b.was_pressed()): # to turn the remote LED off
        radio.send("L") # sends letter L to receiver
    sleep(100)
```

Listing 9-7 shows the MicroPython code you can flash to the micro:bit board (the receiver) connected to the LED. The code will handle all the incoming messages from the remote control (sender) and will write values on the pin attached to the LED.

Listing 9-7. Receiver

```
from microbit import *
import radio

radio.on() # turns the radio on
radio.config(power=7)

pin0.write_digital(0) # turns the LED off on startup

while True:
    message = radio.receive() # read incoming message
    if (message == "H"): # compare incoming message
        pin0.write_digital(1) # turns the LED on
    if (message == "L"):
        pin0.write_digital(0) # turns the LED off
```

After flashing the code onto both micro:bit boards, unplug them from the computer and connect them with batteries. Your micro:bit boards will connect to each other within a few seconds through the radio network (see Figure 9-3).

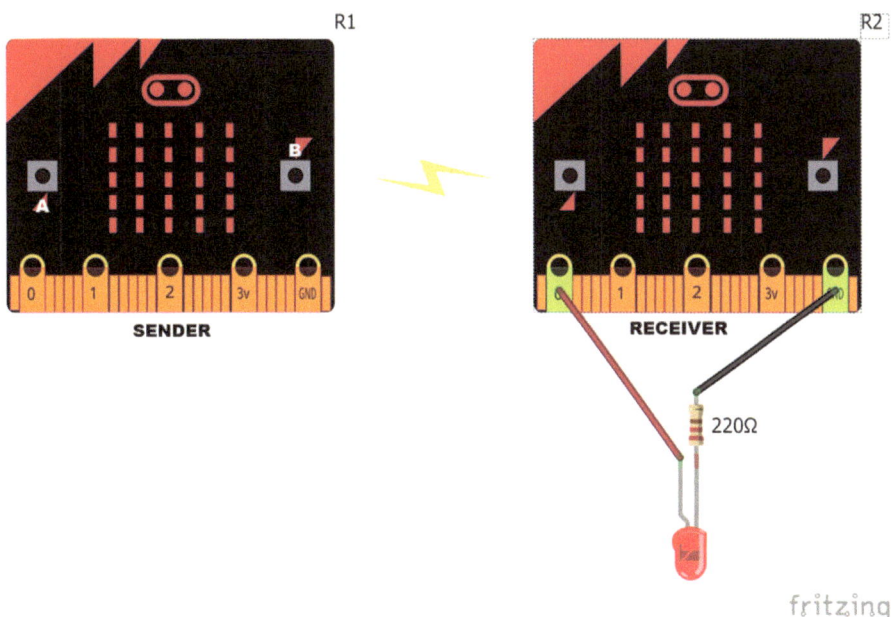

Figure 9-3. Radio network for controlling an LED remotely

Controlling the LED

Table 9-1 shows the list of button events that you can use to control the LED attached to the micro:bit (R2) remotely.

Table 9-1. *Button Events to Control LED Remotely*

Sender (R1)	LED State (R2)
On startup/RESET	OFF
Press and release Button A	ON
Press and release Button B	OFF

199

Building the Wireless Buggy

You can use the micro:bit radio network to control a robot wirelessly by applying the same technique used in the previous section, entitled "Remotely Controlling an LED".

Let's build a simple wireless buggy using the following components.

- One "line following buggy" for the BBC micro:bit

    (`https://www.kitronik.co.uk/5604-line-following-buggy-for-the-bbc-microbit.html`)

- Two micro:bit boards for the buggy and the remote control

- Four AA batteries for the buggy

- Two AA batteries for the remote control

Assembling the Line Following Buggy

A very good tutorial about assembling the line following buggy can be found on Kitronik's blog (`https://www.kitronik.co.uk/blog/bbc-microbit-line-following-buggy/`). You will be using the same instructions, but don't assemble and connect the line following PCB.

After assembling the hardware, connect the two motors to the motor driver board, as instructed here. Figure 9-4 shows the wire connections between the motors and the motor driver board. Label the left motor of the buggy as Motor 1 and the right motor as Motor 2.

- Wire 1 on Motor 1 (white) goes into the `P12` terminal.

- Wire 2 on Motor 1 (green) goes into the `P8` terminal.

- Wire 1 on Motor 2 (blue) goes into the `P0` terminal.

- Wire 2 on Motor 2 (black) goes into the `P16` terminal.

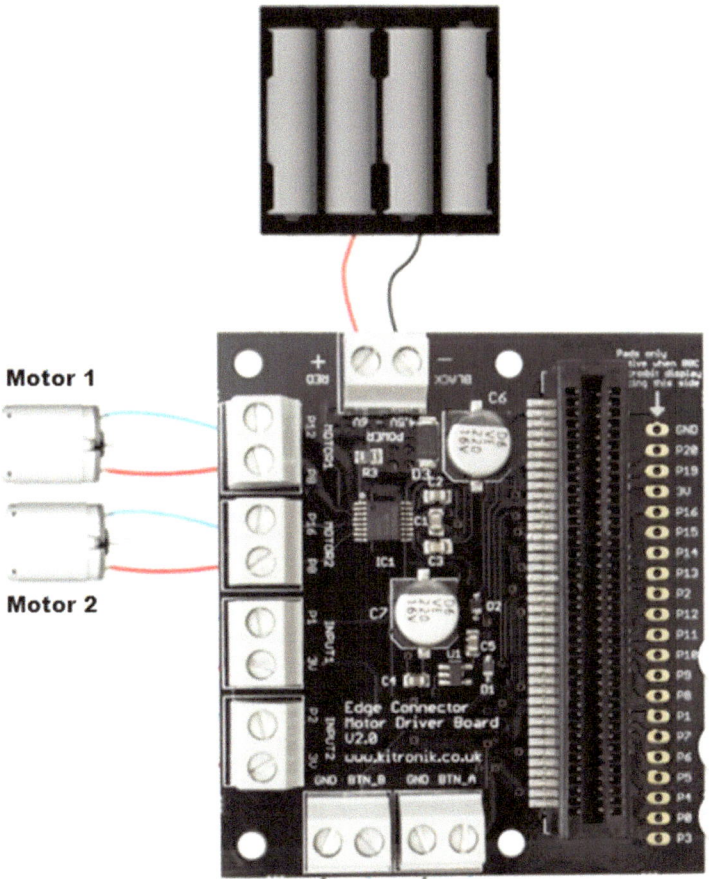

Figure 9-4. *Connecting motors with a motor driver board (image courtesy of Kitronik)*

First, insert the batteries into the buggy's battery case and slide the power switch on the battery case to the OFF position. Then connect the wires from the battery case to the power terminal block on the motor driver board. Use the correct polarity marked on the motor driver board to connect the wires to the terminal block. Figure 9-5 shows the completed chassis.

Figure 9-5. *Completed chassis of the buggy (image courtesy of Kitronik)*

Writing the Code

You can control each motor by writing values on the micro:bit I/O pins connected to them. Tables 9-2 and 9-3 show the input values that can be used to control motors (read https://www.kitronik.co.uk/pdf/5620%20 Motor%20Driver%20Board%20V1.1-2.pdf for more information). However, forward and reverse directions can vary depending on how the motors are connected. You can correct the direction by swapping the two motor wires with the terminal block.

Table 9-2. *Motor Control Pins for Motor 1 (Assume This Is the Left Motor)*

P8	P12	Motor 1 Function
0	0	Coast
1	0	Forward
0	1	Backward
1	1	Brake

Table 9-3. *Motor Control Pins for Motor 2 (Assume This Is the Right Motor)*

P0	P16	Motor 2 Function
0	0	Coast
1	0	Forward
0	1	Backward
1	1	Brake

You can assign the following operations to the built-in buttons on the micro:bit board that you are going to use as the remote control.

- Button A: FORWARD

- Button B: BACKWARD

- Button A+B: BRAKE

Listing 9-8 shows the MicroPython code for the remote control and Listing 9-9 shows the code for the buggy. Write them using the Mu editor and flash to the respective micro:bit boards.

Listing 9-8. Remote Control Code

```
from microbit import *
import radio

radio.on() # turns the radio on
radio.config(power=7)

while True:
    if(button_a.is_pressed()):
        radio.send("F") # FORWARD
    elif(button_b.is_pressed()):
        radio.send("B") # BACKWARD
    elif(button_a.is_pressed() and button_b.is_pressed()):
        radio.send("S") # BRAKE
    else:
        radio.send("C") #COAST
    sleep(100)
```

Listing 9-9. Buggy Code

```
from microbit import *
import radio

radio.on() # turns the radio on
radio.config(power=7)

while True:
    message = radio.receive()
    if (message == "F"): # FORWARD
        pin8.write_digital(1) # motor 1
        pin12.write_digital(0) # motor 1
        pin0.write_digital(1) # motor 2
        pin16.write_digital(0) # motor 2
```

```
if (message == "B"): # BACKWARD
    pin8.write_digital(0) # motor 1
    pin12.write_digital(1) # motor 1
    pin0.write_digital(0) # motor 2
    pin16.write_digital(1) # motor 2
if (message == "S"): # BRAKE
    pin8.write_digital(1) # motor 1
    pin12.write_digital(1) # motor 1
    pin0.write_digital(1) # motor 2
    pin16.write_digital(1) # motor 2
if (message == "C"): # COAST
    pin8.write_digital(0) # motor 1
    pin12.write_digital(0) # motor 1
    pin0.write_digital(0) # motor 2
    pin16.write_digital(0) # motor 2
```

After flashing the code to both micro:bit boards, move the switch on the buggy's battery case to the ON position. Then connect the remote control battery case to the micro:bit you are going to use as the remote control.

Now you're ready to play with your wireless buggy. You can move the buggy forward and backward using built-in buttons A and B. To stop the buggy, press and hold both buttons at the same time. If you haven't pressed any buttons, the buggy will go into coast (neutral) state.

You can improve the design of the buggy by including the following operations.

- *Point turn.* One motor must go forward and the other motor must go backward. The vehicle turns to the side where the motor is going backward.

- *Swing turn.* One motor must stop and the other motor must go backward or forward. There are four types of swing turns: forward left swing turn, backward left swing turn, forward right swing turn, and backward right swing turn.

- Attach additional buttons to the micro:bit and implement code for these turning operations to turn the buggy left and right with different turning mechanisms.

Summary

In this chapter, you learned about the networking features of the micro:bit. Now you know how to build simple applications based on wired and wireless micro:bit networks. The basic knowledge you gained can be applied to build more complex applications, such as data loggers, robots, home automation systems, content delivery systems, and so forth based on the micro:bit networking features.

Throughout this book, you gained foundational knowledge to develop applications for micro:bit with MicroPython. Unfortunately, MicroPython still doesn't support the Bluetooth services provided by the micro:bit. However, you can develop applications with the micro:bit Bluetooth services using the JavaScript Blocks Editor; you can find many resources related to that in the Internet. Appendix B covers the micro:bit Blue app, which you can use with micro:bit Bluetooth services.

APPENDIX A

Updating DAPLink Firmware and Using REPL with Tera Term

This appendix explains how to update the DAPLink firmware on the micro:bit by using maintenance mode. It also shows you how to use REPL (Read-Evaluate-Print-Loop) with Tera Term, a serial terminal program.

DAPLink Firmware

The firmware on the micro:bit is stored inside a separate interface chip called the KL26. This firmware is known as DAPLink. It is the responsibility of this firmware to connect to the USB port and to allow you to drag and drop .hex files that are then programmed into the application processor.

If you want to determine what firmware is loaded in the KL26 interface chip, plug it in and open it in your file manager. Then look inside the details.txt file (see Figure A-1).

© Pradeeka Seneviratne 2018
P. Seneviratne, *Beginning BBC micro:bit*, https://doi.org/10.1007/978-1-4842-3360-3

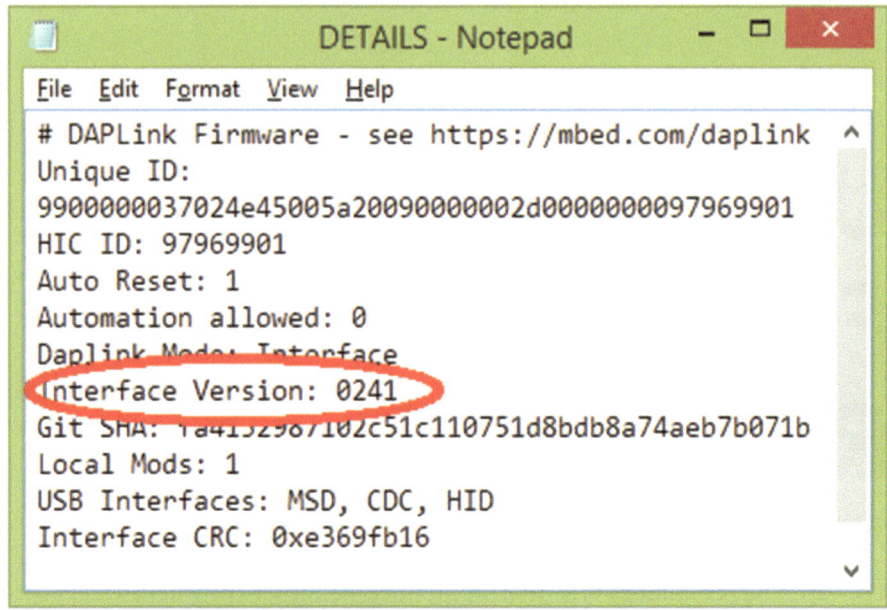

Figure A-1. *The details.txt file contains firmware information*

Updating DAPLink Firmware

You can download the latest DAPLink firmware from `https://github.com/ARMmbed/DAPLink/tags`. At the time of this writing, it was version 0244 (`https://github.com/ARMmbed/DAPLink/releases/tag/0244`).

Note   You should only update the firmware when there is a new DAPLink version available.

The following steps explain how to update the DAPLink firmware on micro:bit.

1. First, bring your micro:bit into maintenance mode. (Read the "Maintenance Mode" section to learn how to bring your micro:bit into maintenance mode.)

2. Copy the firmware (the .hex file) to the `MAINTENANCE` drive.

3. The system LED will start to blink. After the copy operation has completed, the LED will stop blinking and the drive will be dismounted.

4. Unplug the micro:bit from the computer and plug it in again. The micro:bit should appear as `MICROBIT` in the computer's file browser.

Maintenance Mode

Maintenance mode allows you to update the DAPLink firmware, which is an USB interface that allows you to drag and drop binaries onto the target microcontroller. Simply press and hold the RESET button near the micro USB connector while connecting the USB cable to your computer's USB port to enter maintenance mode (see Figure A-2).

Figure A-2. *Preparing micro:bit for MAINTENANCE mode*

Your micro:bit will appear as a mass storage device labeled
MAINTENANCE (see Figure A-3). Sometimes this will happen when you
connect the USB cable to the computer while pressing the RESET button.
You can exit from maintenance mode by unplugging the micro:bit from the
USB and then plugging it back in without pressing the RESET button.

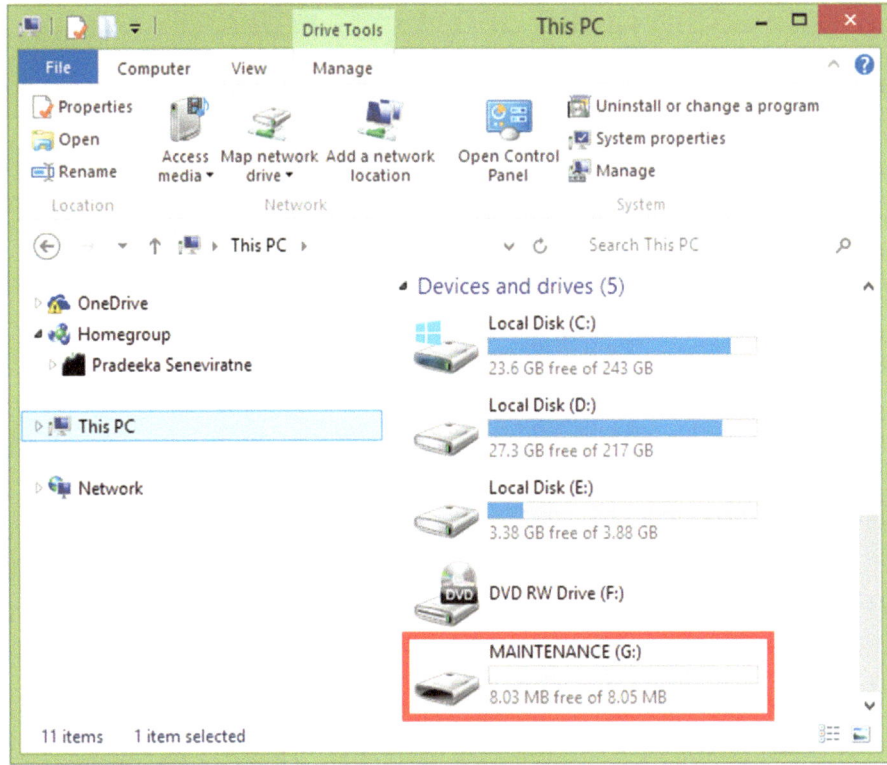

Figure A-3. *micro:bit appears as MAINTENANCE in the file browser in Windows*

Using REPL with Tera Term

REPL (Read-Evaluate-Print-Loop) allows you to run codes line by line without flashing the complete program to the micro:bit. With REPL, you can quickly execute and debug your code while writing. REPL can be performed through a serial connection between the micro:bit and the computer. This section guides you on how to use REPL with Tera Term, which is a serial terminal program in the Windows environment. You can also use REPL with PuTTY or Mu installed on your computer.

Downloading mbed Serial Port Windows Driver

To use REPL with a Windows computer, first you should install the mbed serial port driver. The driver can be downloaded from `https://developer.mbed.org/media/downloads/drivers/mbedWinSerial_16466.exe`. Simply run the downloaded executable file and follow the setup instructions to install it on your Windows OS.

Downloading Tera Term

Tera Term is a very popular serial terminal program that can be used with Windows. It is simple to use and open source. You can read about the Tera Term project by visiting `https://ttssh2.osdn.jp/index.html.en`.

You can download Tera Term for Windows at `https://osdn.net/projects/ttssh2/releases/`. Be sure to download the most recent version. The downloadable files are available in both .exe and .zip formats. The following instructions guide you on how to install Tera Term on Windows and connect the micro:bit from Windows.

1. Run the installer. Choose I Accept the Agreement and click Next.

2. Browse the installation location and click Next.

3. Select Standard Installation from the drop-down list and click Next.

4. Choose your language and click Next. The default language is English.

5. Select Start Menu Folder and click Next.

6. Select Additional Tasks and click Next.

7. Click Install.

8. The setup will install Tera Term on your computer.

9. Select Launch Tera Term and click Finish to complete this process.

Configuring Tera Term

First, you need to configure Tera Term so it can establish the proper communications through the serial port connected to the micro:bit. The following steps explain how to configure Tera Term.

1. Tera Term opens and prompts you for a new connection (see Figure A-4). Select the Serial option and choose the correct COM port from the drop-down list for your micro:bit. Usually, the COM port for your micro:bit is called mbed serial port. Click OK; you should see a blank Tera Term window.

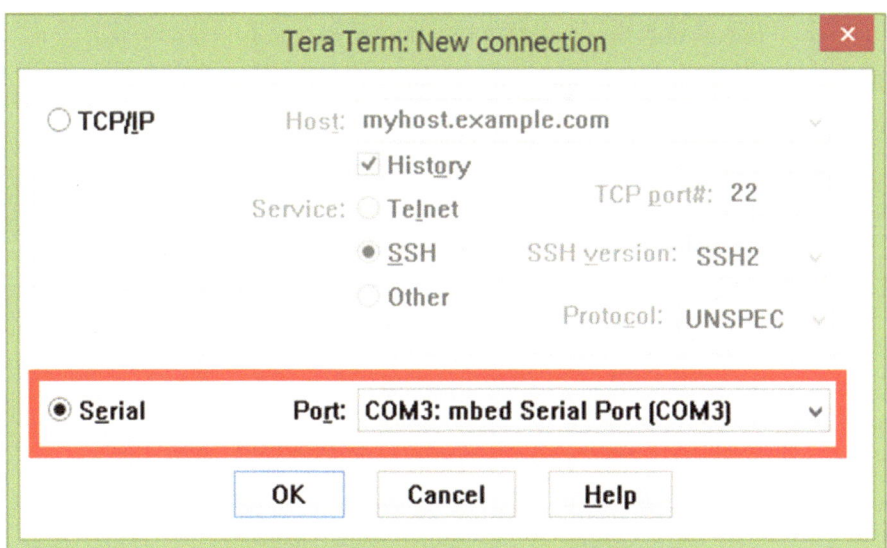

Figure A-4. *Choosing the serial port for micro:bit*

2. Select Terminal from the Setup menu. In the
    Terminal setup dialog box (see Figure A-5), choose
    CR+LF for New-line Receive. Check the Local Echo
    box as well.

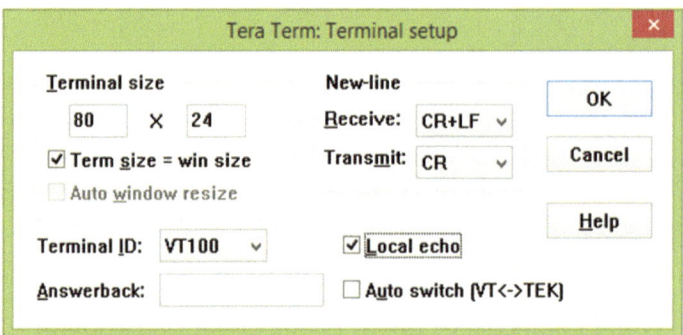

Figure A-5. *Terminal Setup dialog box*

3. Select Serial Port from the Setup menu to confirm
    that the communication settings are correct. In the
    Serial Port Setup dialog box (see Figure A-6), choose
    the Baud rate as 115200. Then click OK to save the
    settings and close the dialog box.

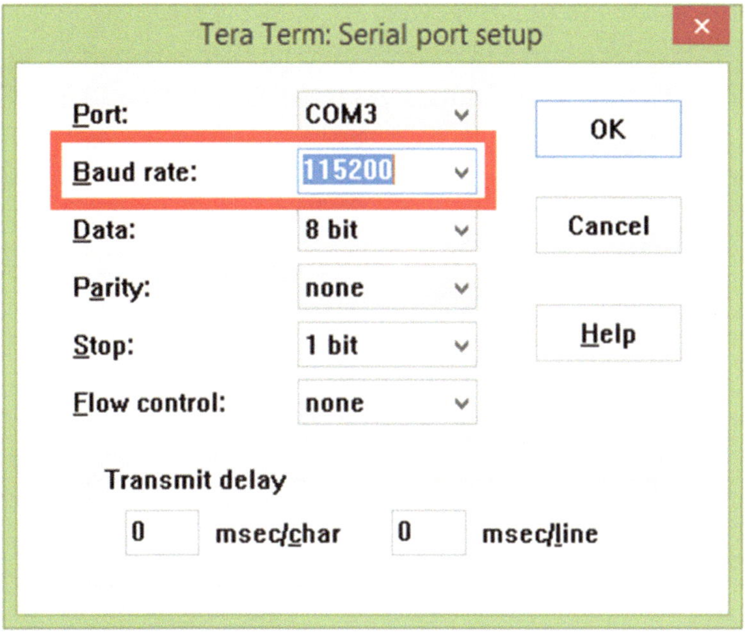

Figure A-6. Serial port setup

4. If you want to permanently save the configuration, select Save Setup from the Setup menu and click the Save button.

Writing MicroPython Code on Tera Term

You can write MicroPython code on a Tera Term window to execute it line-by-line. When you press the Enter key after each line of code, it will execute on micro:bit. Tera Term will store everything you type in a buffer. The following steps explain how to write and execute simple code with Tera Term.

1. Within the Tera Term window, press the Enter key
    to enter command mode. You should see a prompt
    with three greater than signs (see Figure A-7).

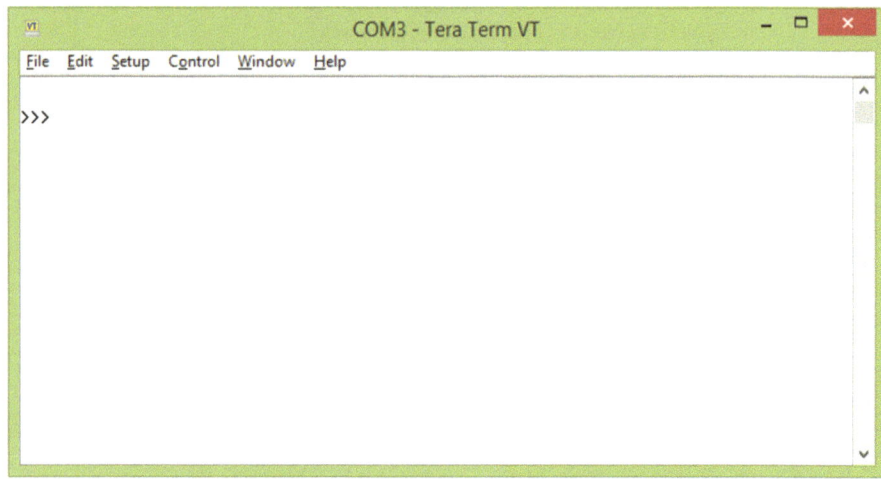

Figure A-7. *Getting to the prompt*

2. First, type the following line of code and press the
    Enter key.

    ```
    import from microbit *
    ```

3. Next, type the following line and press the Enter key
    again (see Figure A-8).

    ```
    display.scroll ('Hello from Tera Term')
    ```

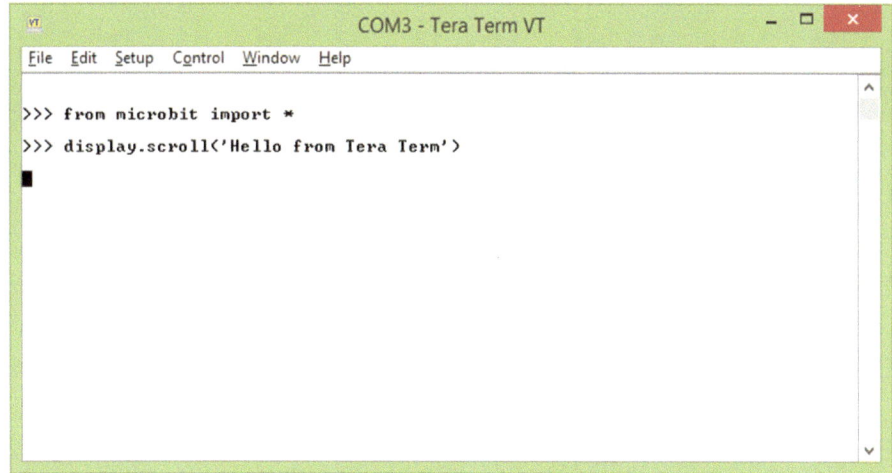

Figure A-8. *Writing code on the Tera Term window*

4. Immediately, the micro:bit will start to scroll the
   'Hello from Tera Term' text on its display.

5. If you want, you can add more lines to this test code.

6. If you want to type a new program, select Clear
   Buffer from the Edit menu.

APPENDIX B

Using micro:bit and micro:bit Blue Apps on Mobile Devices

This appendix presents how to use micro:bit and micro:bit Blue apps on mobile devices to work with micro:bit. These apps act as a Bluetooth bridge between the micro:bit and the mobile device. Each app has its own advantages and disadvantages. However, they allow you to get more out of the micro:bit. Let's explore the micro:bit and micro:bit Blue apps.

Using the micro:bit App

The micro:bit app allows you to create code, flash the resulting .hex file onto micro:bit and interface with device components of the mobile device such as the camera.

You can download the official micro:bit app for Android, developed by Samsung Electronics UK at Google Play (`https://play.google.com/store/apps/details?id=com.samsung.microbit`). This will require Android 4.4. or higher installed on your mobile device.

© Pradeeka Seneviratne 2018
P. Seneviratne, *Beginning BBC micro:bit*, https://doi.org/10.1007/978-1-4842-3360-3

If you have an Apple iPhone or iPad, you can download the micro:bit app from the iTunes App Store at `https://itunes.apple.com/gb/app/micro-bit/id1092687276?mt=8`. The micro:bit app for iOS is currently compatible with a wide range of iPhone and iPad devices with different combinations of component hardware and iOS versions. The list of compatible devices can be found on the app's download page.

Pairing with micro:bit

The pairing process is fun and easy with both the official Android and the iOS app. First apply power to your micro:bit using two 1.5V AA batteries.

The following steps guide you on how to pair your micro:bit with a mobile device. The images shown in this section are from a mobile phone with Android OS. The same steps can be applied to devices using iOS.

1.   Open the micro:bit app.

2. Tap the Connect button (see Figure B-1).

Figure B-1. *Tapping the Connect button*

3. Tap the PAIR A NEW MICRO:BIT button (see
    Figure B-2).

Figure B-2. *Tapping the PAIR A NEW MICRO:BIT button*

4. Turn on the Bluetooth of your mobile device if you
    haven't done so already (see Figure B-3).

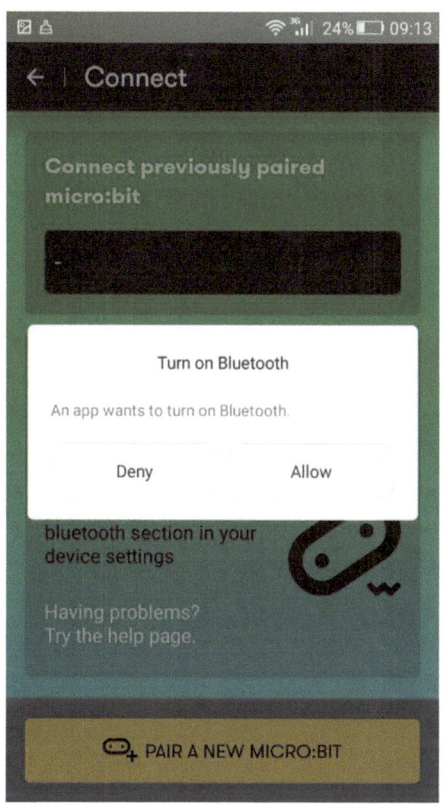

Figure B-3. *Turning on Bluetooth*

5.   The app prompts you to hold the built-in A and B
     buttons, then press and release the RESET button
     (see Figure B-4).

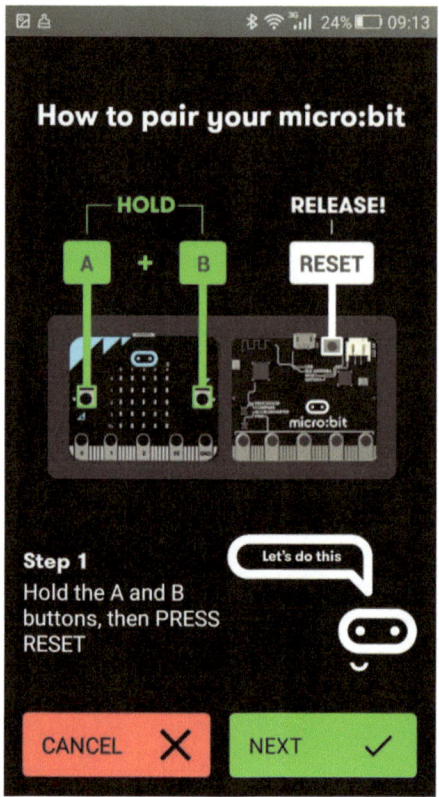

Figure B-4. *Pairing step 1*

6.   The text PAIRING MODE will scroll along the micro:bit
     LED display.

7.   Tap NEXT on the app.

8. The micro:bit will display a pattern on the LED
    display, and the app will show an empty grid. Now
    copy the pattern from your micro:bit onto the grid
    of the app. If you have created the same pattern on
    the grid, the app displays the message `Ooh, pretty!`
    (see Figure B-5). Then tap the PAIR button to pair
    the micro:bit with the mobile device.

Figure B-5. *Pairing step 2*

9. A left arrow will blink on the LED display to prompt you to press the A button. When you press the A button, a series of numbers will display on the LED screen. This is the pairing key that's used to authenticate both devices. Meanwhile, a notification will arrive to your mobile device that prompts you to enter the same key. Now enter the key in the text box and tap OK to proceed.

10. If you entered the same key, you will get the message shown in Figure B-6.

Figure B-6. *Message saying you have successfully paired with micro:bit*

11. Press the RESET button on the micro:bit to complete
     the setup.

12. You can reconnect your micro:bit to the app at
     any time by tapping the name (i.e., PEVUP) of your
     micro:bit listed under Connect Previously Paired
     micro:bit (see Figure B-7).

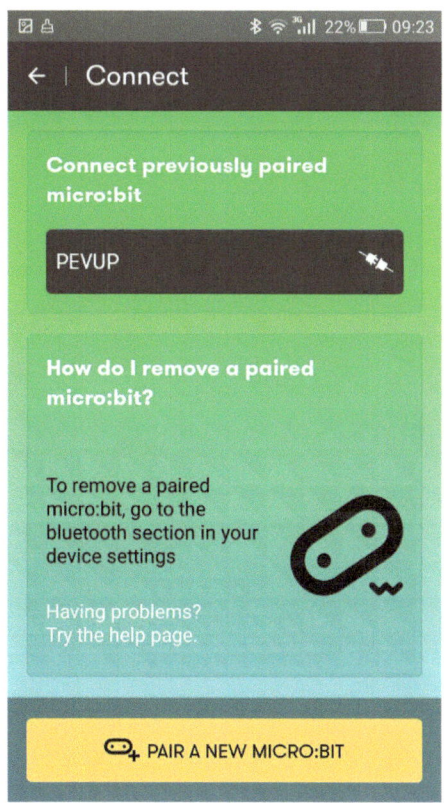

Figure B-7. *Reconnect to the previously paired micro:bit*

Writing Code with micro:bit App

Now you are ready to create code with the micro:bit app. The app allows you to flash the code to the micro:bit from your mobile device through Bluetooth connectivity.

1. Go to the micro:bit app's main page and tap the Flash button (see Figure B-8).

Figure B-8. *Tapping the Flash button*

2.   Then tap the MY SCRIPTS button (see Figure B-9).

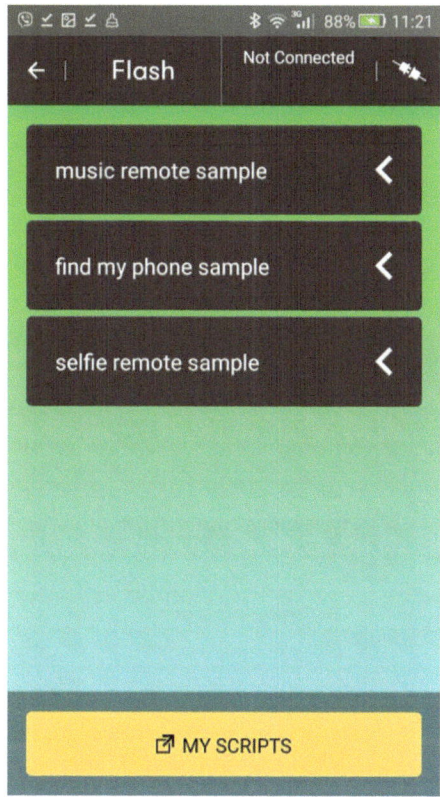

Figure B-9. *Tapping the MY SCRIPTS button*

3. Tap the Create Code button (see Figure B-10) from
    the list to create a new script.

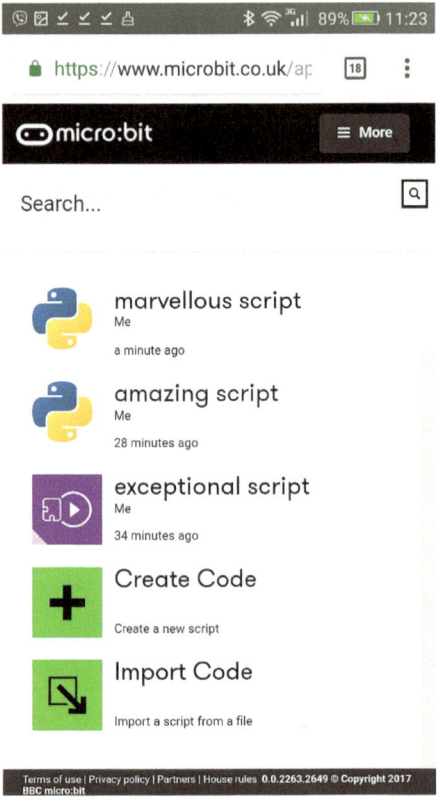

Figure B-10. *Tapping the Create Code button*

Creating MicroPython Code with the micro:bit App

The app allows you to choose following code editors to create code for
micro:bit.

- JavaScript
- Block Editor

- Touch Develop

- MicroPython

The following steps guide you on how to create simple code with MicroPython and flash it to the micro:bit through the micro:bit app.

1. Tap the MicroPython option (see Figure B-11) from the list of code editors.

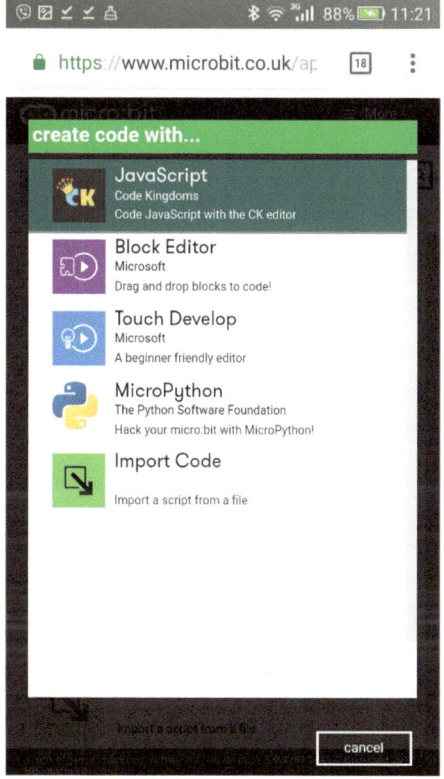

Figure B-11. *Tapping the MicroPython editor option*

2. The MicroPython editor will open with default code (see Figure B-12). This is the same MicroPython editor that you explored in Chapter 1. Note that this editor is not a part of the micro:bit app and can be directly accessed at https://www.microbit.co.uk/app.

Figure B-12. *MicroPython editor*

3. Let's flash the default MicroPython code to the
    micro:bit. To do so, tap the Download button on
    the editor's toolbar (see Figure B-13). The .hex
    file for the MicroPython code will download to
    the downloads folder of your mobile device (i.e.,
    marvelous_script.hex). Also, the micro:bit app can
    access the downloaded .hex files directly from the
    downloads folder of your mobile device.

Figure B-13. *Downloading a .hex file for the code*

4. Now go to the main page of the micro:bit app and tap the Flash button. The app will show all the downloaded .hex files as a list, so you can flash them to the micro:bit by tapping the FLASH button associated with the file name (i.e., marvelous_script) (see Figure B-14).

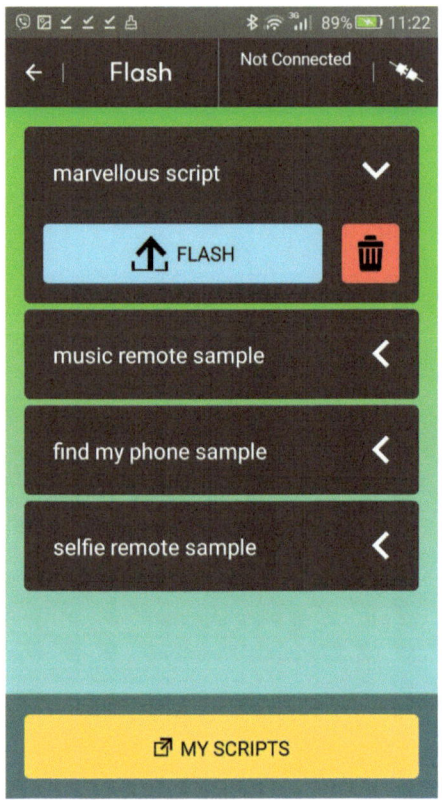

Figure B-14. *List of .hex files for flashing*

5. The app will start to flash the code into the micro:bit
    board with the Bluetooth connectivity. Turn on the
    Bluetooth on your mobile device if you're prompted
    by tapping the Allow button (see Figure B-15).

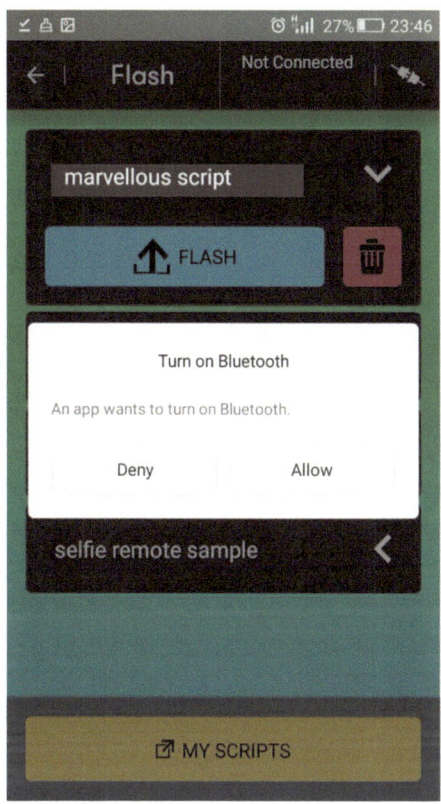

Figure B-15. *Turning on Bluetooth*

6. Tap the OK button to confirm the flashing (see
    Figure B-16).

Figure B-16. *Confirmation screen for flashing*

7. The app will start to flash the code to the micro:bit. Don't try to interact with the micro:bit board during the flashing process (see Figure B-17).

Figure B-17. *Flashing in progress*

8. Tap the OK button to disconnect the micro:bit board from the app (see Figure B-18).

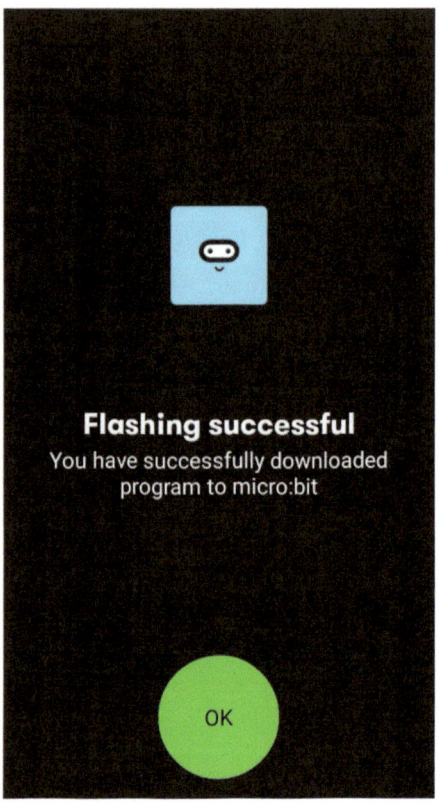

Figure B-18. *Flashing successful message*

9. If you want to reconnect the app to the micro:bit
    board, tap the OK button (see Figure B-19).

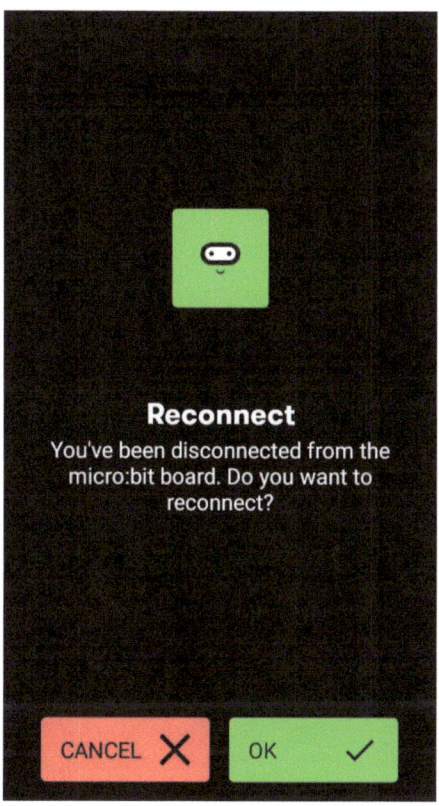

Figure B-19. *The Reconnect screen*

Note   Sometimes, using the micro:bit app to flash code to micro:bit
over Bluetooth isn't successful.

Using the micro:bit Blue App

The micro:bit Blue app contains a series of demonstrations that use the BBC micro:bit Bluetooth profile in various ways. Its purpose is to act as a demo and to provide a source of example code that shows you how to use the Bluetooth profile from Android. This app is originally developed by Martin Woolley and currently available for Android.

Installing micro:bit Blue

You can install micro:bit Blue from Google Play (see Figure B-20).

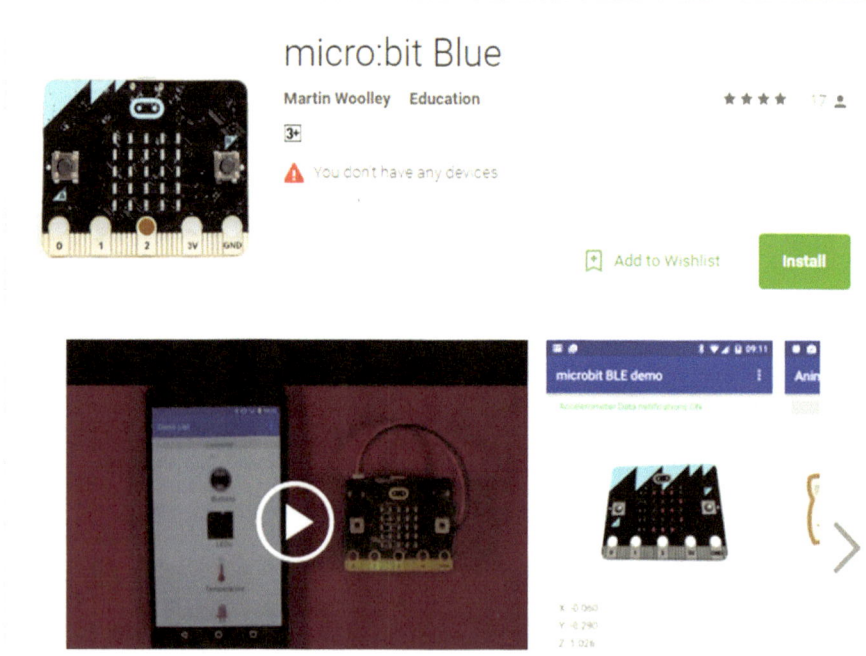

Figure B-20. *Micro:bit Blue at Google Play*

Entering Pairing Mode

Before pairing your micro:bit with your phone or tablet, you should enter your micro:bit board into pairing mode. Follow these steps to enter pairing mode.

1. Hold down buttons A and B on the front of your micro:bit at the same time.

2. While still holding down buttons A and B, press and then release the RESET button on the back of the micro:bit. Keep holding down buttons A and B.

3. You should see the message **'PAIRING MODE!'** start to scroll across the micro:bit display. When you see this message, you can release the buttons.

4. Eventually you'll see a strange pattern on your micro:bit display. This is like your micro:bit's signature. Other people's micro:bits will probably display a different pattern.

Your micro:bit is now ready to be paired with the other device.

Pairing Your micro:bit with Your Android Phone or Tablet

With the pairing mode, you can pair your micro:bit board with your phone or tablet using the Bluetooth screen within the Android's Settings screen. The following steps guide you on how to do this with common smartphones and tablets.

1. Go into Settings.

2. Select Bluetooth.

3. Switch your micro:bit into pairing mode using the steps in the previous section.

4. Wait until 'PAIRING MODE!' has finished scrolling across the micro:bit display. You should see your micro:bit listed on your Android smartphone under the "Available Devices" heading with a name something like micro:bit [pevup]. Note that the five characters in brackets at the end will vary.

5. On the Android smartphone, tap the micro:bit named in the Available Devices list (see Figure B-21). This will initiate the pairing process.

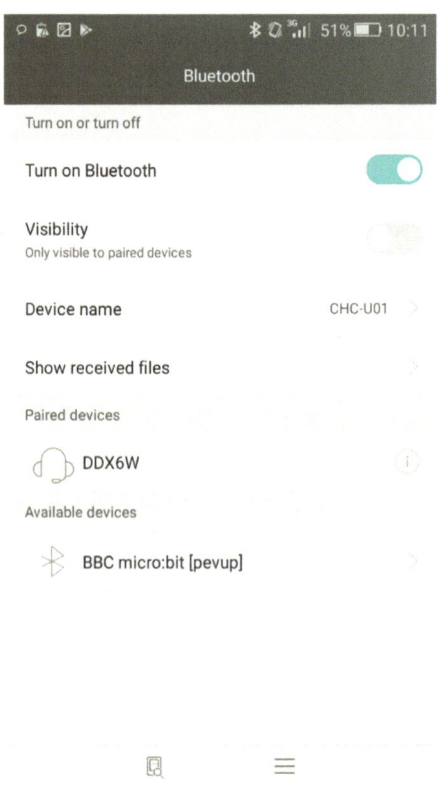

Figure B-21. *The micro:bit is under the Available Devices list (image captured from a Huawei CHC-U0I phone)*

6. The micro:bit will display a left pointing arrow and
    the Android smartphone will pop up a box into
    which you will be invited to enter a PIN (a Personal
    Identification Number).

7. Press button A on the micro:bit and watch carefully
    as the micro:bit displays a sequence of six random
    numbers. You may find it easier to write them down
    than to remember them.

8. Enter the six digits that the micro:bit displayed
    on your Android smartphone in the pop-up box
    provided. Select Done. See Figure B-22.

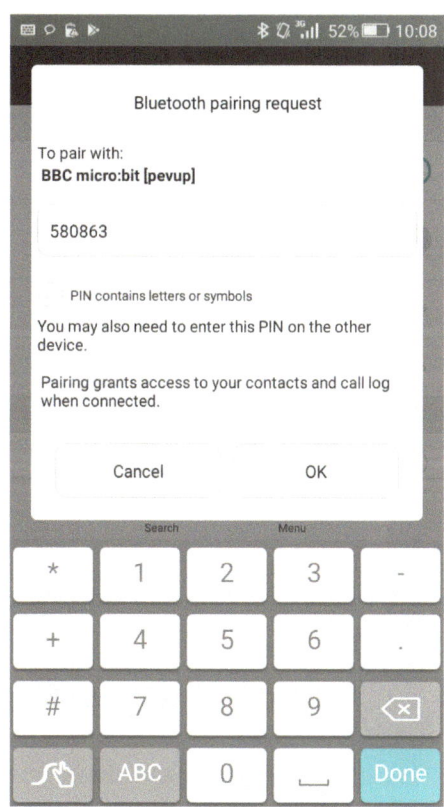

Figure B-22. *Pairing the PIN (image captured from a Huawei CHC-U0I phone)*

9. If you entered the right numbers, the micro:bit will
    display a tick/check mark. If you made a mistake, it
    will display a cross or X and you should try again.

Using the App

Open the app by tapping the micro:bit blue icon on your Android screen.
Then, you must connect your paired micro:bit board to the micro:bit blue app.

1. Tap the FIND PAIRED BBC MICRO BIT(S) button
    at the bottom of the screen (see Figure B-23). The
    app will start to scan for paired micro:bit boards and
    display them on the screen.

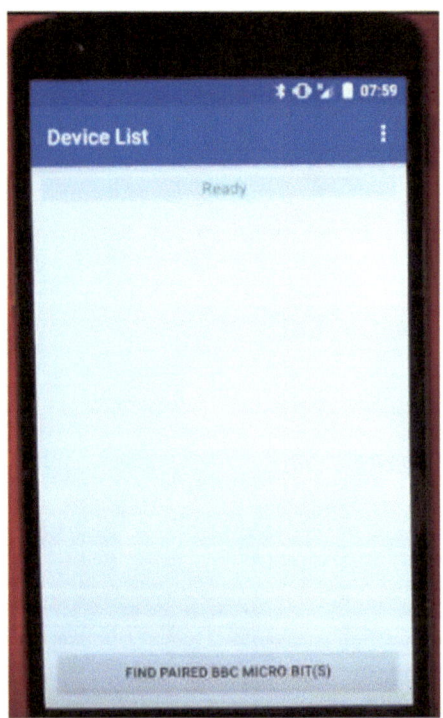

Figure B-23. *Finding paired micro:bit(s)*

2. Tap the name of your micro:bit board from the list of names (see Figure B-24).

Figure B-24. *List of paired micro:bit(s)*

3. The app will show the Demo list. The Demo list
    includes the following sample projects, which use
    the micro:bit Bluetooth profile.

    •   Accelerometer

    •   Magnetometer

    •   Buttons

    •   LEDs

    •   Temperature

    •   I/O Digital Output

    •   Temperature Alarm

    •   Squirrel Counter

    •   Device Information

    •   Animal Magic

    •   Dual D-Pad Counter

    •   Heart Rate Histogram

    •   Animal Vegetable Mineral

    •   Trivia Scoreboard

You can open any demo program by tapping its demo icon. As an
example, open the LEDs demo program from the list. The LED demo
allows you to draw an image or display text on the LED display.

1. Under the Demo list, tap LEDs (see Figure B-25).

Figure B-25. *Demo list*

2. You will get the screen shown in Figure B-26.

Figure B-26. *Settings page for LED display*

3. The screen has two sections. The first section allows
    you to draw any image on the LED display. You can
    tap any square to create a new image. After creating
    the image, tap SET DISPLAY. You can see the new
    image on the micro:bit's LED display.

4. Then type new text under the Display text by
    replacing the default Hello!. Then tap the SEND
    TEXT button. You can see the new text start to scroll
    on the LED display.

    When you try a demo program, the micro: bit blue
    doesn't flash any code to your micro:bit board. You
    can press the RESET button on the micro:bit to exit
    from the program and use the previously flashed
    program.

Index

A

Accelerometer
  NXP/Freescale MMA8652 chip, 109–110
  overall, 115–116
  reading
    movement in x, y, z planes, 112
    three axes, 110–114
    tuples, 113
  spirit level, 114–115
Analog I/O, 85–87

B

Beats, 150
Buttons
  handling user inputs
    get_presses() method, 65
    is_pressed() method, 63
    methods, 62
    was_pressed() method, 65
  momentary pushbutton
    external buttons, 68
    GPIO pins, 70
    internal connection, 67
    pinout, 67
    read_digital() method, 73
  pushbuttons, 61–62

C

Compass
  calibrating, 123–124
  heading, 126–130
  magnetic field, x and y axes, 124–126
  NXP/Freescale MAG3110 chip, 122

D

DAPLink firmware
  details.txt file, 207–208
  KL26 interface chip, 207
  maintenance mode, 209–211
  update, 208–209
Digital I/O, 87–89

E

Earphones, 141–143
Edge connector, I/O pins
  analog, 85–87
  breakout board
    BBC micro, 77
    I2C pins, 77
    inserting micro, 78–79
    pin headers, 78
    prototyping area, 78

O

Get the eBook for only $5!

Why limit yourself?

With most of our titles available in both PDF and ePUB format, you can access your content wherever and however you wish—on your PC, phone, tablet, or reader.

Since you've purchased this print book, we are happy to offer you the eBook for just $5.

To learn more, go to http://www.apress.com/companion or contact support@apress.com.

Apress®